KIM ZMESKAL
DETERMINATION TO WIN

A Biography by Krista Quiner

THE BRADFORD BOOK COMPANY
East Hanover, New Jersey

Printed in the United States of America
October 1994
10 9 8 7 6 5

Photo Credits:
All photographs and artwork were produced by Steve Lange

Library of Congress Cataloging-in-Publication Number: 94-79473

ISBN: 0-9643460-0-1

For my husband Barry,
who has put much time and effort into my dream

To my sister Cara,
who is the writer of the family and a great gymnast

To Kim Zmeskal,
whose dedication to gymnastics inspired this book

ACKNOWLEDGMENTS

To Barry Quiner, without whose editorial guidance and attention to detail this could not have happened;

To Cara Bailey, who critiqued the manuscript with the touch of a true journalist;

To Keith and Judy Bailey, whose support and encouragement were essential and immeasurable;

To Steve Lange, who was very kind, easy to work with, and generous with his hobby and computer expertise;

To Dwight Normile, who went beyond his duties by offering suggestions;

To Mark and Paul Quiner, whose advice was invaluable;

To Paul "Buddy" Kelchner and Shields Gymnastics, who supplied valuable resource materials;

To Jennifer Korbo, who willingly relinquished the use of her computer many times for the project;

To the Denville and East Hanover Libraries, whose friendly and pleasant staffs were very helpful;

I owe sincere *thanks*.

Krista Quiner

FOREWORD

Although few recall exactly where Kim Zmeskal finished at the 1992 Olympics (10th), most will remember her more for that competition than any other. Barcelona was to be the crowning glory to her career and, in a way, legitimize her World Championships victory the year before in Indianapolis. Doubters and foes alike waited to see how she would fare on neutral ground, which, if you think about it, does not exist in gymnastics.

As it happened, scores had little to do with Zmeskal's Barcelona results. She did not win. Didn't even come close. She admitted to having a bad meet but not to being injured. Fact is, Zmeskal had sustained a stress fracture in her left leg just prior to the Games. The cruel timing of the injury left her less than 100 percent at a time when she needed everything she had. Afterward, Zmeskal still offered no excuse. That's not her style.

That Zmeskal could draw so much attention prior to those Olympics is testament to her achievements as a competitor. In April of '92 Zmeskal put her reputation on the line at the first—and last—Individual Apparatus World Championships in Paris. Sure, nobody could take away her all-around title there, but skeptics would certainly be satisfied if Zmeskal took a sound drubbing from the likes of Svetlana Boginskaya, Henrietta Onodi, and others.

After three arduous rounds of competition, Zmeskal proved herself to the world—again—with golds on balance beam and floor exercise. In effect, she won the all-around in Paris, even though there was no medal for it.

Although the Paris event hardly received the usual hype given other world championships, Zmeskal's performances there elevated her status nonetheless. For all of her competitive accomplishments, Zmeskal can savor her Paris triumphs as much as those from any other competition, maybe more. She was a better gymnast in Paris than she had been in Indianapolis. And she kept improving as Barcelona approached.

Kim Zmeskal should not be remembered solely for the '92 Olympics—nor for any other single competition. Zmeskal's career is exemplary more for the personal characteristics she displayed than for any athletic feats she accomplished on the beam or bars. In the span of a year, Zmeskal endured with equal grace the suffocating pressures of winning and losing on a world stage. That's a lot to handle at any age, let alone when you're in your mid-teens.

Unlike so many athletes today, Zmeskal is comfortable with herself and knows down deep that her identity will never stem from competitive results. Indianapolis didn't improve her, Barcelona could never ruin her.

After a two-year layoff, Zmeskal announced her plans to return to competitive gymnastics. She hopes to compete in the 1996 Atlanta Olympics. But she's not doing it to fill a void left by Barcelona, to change the past. What's done is done. She still loves the sport that has been her life. Through the years, good and bad, Zmeskal's determination to succeed has remained constant.

By chance, I sat next to Kim at the 1994 USA Championships in Nashville, Tennessee. (With a guest pass, she was seated in the press section.) It was interesting for me to see her as a spectator instead of a competitor. Throughout the evening, she cheered for virtually every gymnast in the meet. Only words of praise and encouragement left her lips. Impressive, I thought, for someone with such competitive drive of her own.

But what else would you expect from someone like Kim? She's the perfect example of an athlete who participates in sports for all the right reasons. And because of that, Kim Zmeskal is a winner, on and off the apparatus.

—**Dwight Normile**
Editor, *International Gymnast* magazine

CONTENTS

1. The Little Tiger   1

2. Beating the Competition   16

3. The National Champion   35

4. Problems with Bela   56

5. Conquering the World   79

6. Silencing the Skeptics   102

7. Making the Dream Team   116

8. The Fall   135

9. Battle for the Gold   151

10. A Comeback   164

Notes   189
About the Author   199

Chapter 1

THE LITTLE TIGER

It is the beginning of another hot summer day in Houston, Texas. Soon the air will be sweltering with humidity. Early in the morning, only a little after seven o'clock, most of the city is just awakening.

On the north side of town, a few cars are parked outside a building that could pass for a warehouse. Inside, bright sunlight shines through tiny windows. Several small girls are on a row of balance beams, each traveling the length of the beam only to turn and travel back. Like robots, they perform with precision the same movements, back and forth, over and over. Reaching the end of the beam again, the girls perform full turns, each finishing by holding one leg in the air. The watchful instructor makes a correction where necessary, then the girls do it again. Then again. There is no noise except for the voice of the coach and the thud of feet against the padded beams.

KIM ZMESKAL

Sweat streams down the body of one tiny girl from her head to her calves. Dusted with chalk and wearing a colorful leotard, she performs the seemingly endless repetitions with the rest of the girls, occasionally pausing to wipe the perspiration from her brow and tighten her damp ponytail. She is a scrawny thirteen-year-old who still needs to develop some muscles, but her slight frame disguises tremendous strength. She executes a back handspring and wobbles slightly; she comes down hard on herself, determined to do it better the next time. To make it perfect.

This girl has been in the system since she was very young. Her coach has been grooming her and several others to be the next superstars in gymnastics. She has been working in silence and waiting for her turn to be the champion, knowing her time will come.

She thrives on competition. "She is like a wild animal," her coach says. "Biting, catching, flying. Bam! Pow!"[1] This girl wants to be the best. Her goal is to win the gold medal in the 1992 Olympics in Barcelona, Spain, and she is willing to work for it at all costs, to sacrifice her childhood for a shiny medal hanging from a brightly-colored ribbon.

The media has not paid attention to her; its focus has always been on the top athletes of the gym, those constantly in the spotlight. The cameras have followed the older girls, and the younger ones have seemed almost invisible. But now, the seasoned veterans have all departed. Some have retired and gone home, while others have sought training elsewhere. One by one they have gone, leaving only the little ones.

With the departure of the experienced competitors, the instructor hopes to usher in his next generation of talented individuals to carry the American torch. These girls will be the new pride and joy of the club, the ones he has shaped and molded both mentally and physically over the past seven years.

These miniature-sized athletes, all barely teenagers and little more than four feet tall, have been pushed to the forefront of American gymnastics. They are the United States' best hope for the future.

And leading the pack, this tiny girl on the balance beam. This tenacious little fighter with the soul of a tiger and the determination to win.

This is her story.

* * *

Kimberly Lynn Zmeskal was born in Houston, Texas, on February 6, 1976—a few months before Nadia Comaneci won her gold medals in Montreal under a Romanian coach named Bela Karolyi.

Kim was an energetic little girl. Her mom could not keep her still as a child. Kim confessed that she liked to "just run around" as a youngster. Strawberry blonde-haired, blue-eyed Kim always seemed to be landing on her head or trying to stand on it.

"My mom says that when I was little, I liked jumping on the couch all the time," Kim said. "We had a trampoline and we used to set it up behind the couch, and I used to jump over the couch." Since she never knocked over a lamp, her parents did not discourage her.

Kim's first exposure to gymnastics was as a spectator. "I was six years old when I started," Kim recalled. "The reason I did was that my parents both work, so I had to stay at a babysitter's house. Her daughter was enrolled at the gym, and I always used to have to go watch. I got tired of watching and told them I wanted to start doing it, too."[2]

Kim remembered her first years in gymnastics: "My journey . . . began here in Houston at Karolyi's gym, only I started before Bela was even here. I started gymnastics when I was six and Bela came about a year later."[3]

Bela Karolyi, Kim's coach, grew up in Transylvania, Romania. Bela was very athletic. He was successful at boxing and was a Junior National Champion in the hammer throw. However, there was one sport he could not master: gymnastics. He failed a required course in gymnastics at the University in Bucharest.

Bela was determined to succeed, so he practiced the skills until he could do them well. He made the collegiate gymnastics team and won the heart of a fellow gymnast, Martha Eross. They were married in 1963 and shortly thereafter opened a gym together. It was there that they found and developed their star pupil, Nadia Comaneci, who went on to win the 1976 Olympics and place a controversial second in the 1980 Olympics.

Bela defected to the United States in March 1981 because of political problems he was having with the Romanian government. Bela had little money when he and his wife first moved to the United States. He knew six languages, but unfortunately English was not one of them. Bela had to work odd jobs, like cleaning and sweeping sleazy bars and restaurants along a waterfront during the early morning, just to earn enough money to survive. He and his wife would stay in the cheapest hotels, and he would sometimes have to walk three hours to and from work. His meager wages, for which he negotiated in very broken English, would sometimes buy only a soft pretzel that he and his wife would share for a meal.

Bela was a hard worker by nature and hoped that, instead of mopping floors, he would be able to focus his intensity and talents on American gymnasts. He tried to find work in the gymnastics community, but no one wanted the competition he would bring.

"At first, you feel anger," Bela said bitterly. "I thought,

'Who needs this? Why not go back and face it in Romania?' But finally, you start to drop that pride. Just like an animal, when you want to survive, you don't think anymore."

Eventually, Bela contacted a friend in Oklahoma, Paul Ziert, who was surprised to hear of Bela's plight. He gave Bela and his wife jobs, and after awhile they had saved enough money to buy a gym in Houston, Texas, that was about to fold.[4]

Kim was among the first two hundred students to sign up when Bela took over the ailing gym in 1982. Bela also received a budding young talent from Fairmont, West Virginia, who went on to win the most coveted prize in gymnastics—the Olympic all-around title—in 1984. Her name was Mary Lou Retton, and with Bela's guidance she became an overnight success. In Mary Lou, Bela created his second Olympic Champion, only this time he did it with an American. And wide-eyed little Kim paid close attention to everything that happened.

Kim had watched Mary Lou's rigorous training schedule at Karolyi's gym for a year and a half prior to the Olympics in 1984. Kim looked up to Mary Lou; she was Kim's idol and inspiration.

"When I was eight years old, Mary Lou Retton won the Olympic all-around gold medal," Kim said. "Since she also trained at Karolyi's, I was able to watch her all the time. Mary Lou is the person who planted the dream inside of me to want to become a world-level gymnast!"[5]

Bela and Martha first noticed Kim about a year after they took over the Houston gym. "I believe she was about eight years old when we saw her for the first time," Bela recalled. "Yes, [it was] a little test, a little contest, a little Saturday/ Sunday races. 'Oh, there's a little tiger over there. She wants to beat one, she wants to beat the other one, she wants to be a winner.' So that's the first time I notice her. 'Yeah, that little girl might grow into a good gymnast.'"[6]

A good gymnast maybe, Bela reasoned, but he had his doubts about anything more than that. "At the beginning, it didn't look like Kim would develop into a great gymnast," he said. "The only thing evident to me . . . was her natural speed. Her little legs could move so fast that her heels looked like a blur as they pumped up and down. When she ran toward the horse her speed was incredible."

Bela said that Kim stood out in his mind for a couple of reasons. "Kim was legendary for her falls," he pointed out. "She'd fall regularly from the beam during a routine. She was like popcorn popping on and off. And most of the time she'd mess up her floor routines by over-rotating her somersaults."

Another of Kim's characteristics was first noticed by Martha. "Bela," she said to her husband one afternoon, "have you noticed that as soon as you step into the gym, the first one to jump up to an event and do something more than she has ever done before is Kim?"[7]

Bela realized that his wife was correct. Kim was always the one seeking attention and trying to perform for those whom she considered important. From then on Bela paid closer attention to the little girl he nicknamed Kimbo.

Bela had always been more interested in the child with the proper attitude, the one who was excited by the sport and wanted to get ahead of the rest, than the super-talented athlete who typically did not have the patience to learn the skills or the ability to work hard.

Kim's fierce competitive drive and determination had caught Bela's eye. She was a fighter, although she did not show it in her face.

"Her personality," Bela said, "which you otherwise cannot figure out talking to her, you would never, never pick it up from her little sleepy cat-face what kind of little tiger [she] is in essence, and in reality, and it really comes out only when the competition starts."[8]

Recognizing her ability, Bela placed her on the training squad for talented young individuals called the Hope Group.

"I was in the original Hope Group," Kim explained. "It was a group which Bela and Martha selected after looking at all the girls at about the age of seven or eight."[9]

Mary Lou remembered a little munchkin named Kim running around. "Kim—you could just tell—had the talent, had the potential, and she had that drive; you could see it in her face," Mary Lou said with a smile. "Bela used to call her the Little Pumpkin. She was on our little tiny tot Hope Team, so when her time came she was going to be the champion."[10]

Kim showed much promise, and Bela elected Kim president of his Pumpkin Generation. He used this name for his newest little sensations because, as he described, they were "such cute little kids, and an adorable bunch."

Kim wanted to get better, so she practiced her moves at home. She tried to learn her splits and improve her flexibility since this was a weak area for her.

"I would practice them even while watching television,"[11] she said.

Kim was a right-sided gymnast. That means she performed cartwheels, roundoffs, splits, and turns to the right side. She placed her right hand down first on her cartwheel and roundoff. She favored splits where her right leg was in front. She also wrote and signed autographs, when necessary, with her right hand.

Kim used to jump on the trampoline at her home and pretend she was Mary Lou Retton, not knowing that someday other little girls would make believe they were Kim Zmeskal. Even after winning the Olympics, Mary Lou still came into the gym to try to win her third consecutive American Cup title in early 1985. She encouraged the younger gymnasts and gave them advice.

"She's [Mary Lou] told me that it's going to be hard the next couple of years," said Kim, "but that I have to keep going with my goals and that I can accomplish them if I work hard enough."[12]

Kim had the look of the emerging style of gymnast that Mary Lou had created. Even at a young age the similarities between Kim and Mary Lou were evident.

"Look at your little sister," Bela used to say to Mary Lou when referring to Kim.

Mary Lou saw the resemblance: "She was always so strong and gutsy. I remember thinking, 'Hey, she's a lot like me. I think she's going to be a great gymnast someday.'"[13]

Both Kim and Mary Lou had short, strong-looking bodies. Their calf muscles were round and compact, built for quickness and power, unlike the oval and elongated calves of endurance runners. Kim and Mary Lou were also more stocky in build than the lean, long-lined gymnasts like Shannon Miller and Julianne McNamara.

"I'm probably more the powerful type like Mary Lou, than a dancer,"[14] Kim admitted.

Kim's height was an added advantage in gymnastics. It was easier to learn to flip and twist being small. At the age of nine, Kim was only three feet ten inches tall.

Kim first began competing seriously at age ten, four years after starting gymnastics. By the time Kim was eleven years old she was a Class I gymnast.

The gymnastics class system was a little different back then. Class IV was the lowest and Class I was the highest. Beyond Class I was a special group called Elite, the ultimate ranking possible. Nowadays, there are ten levels and Elite.

Level 1 is the lowest and Level 10 is the highest besides Elite.
Many gymnasts do not aspire to be an Elite. A Level 8 or 9
gymnast may be capable of receiving a college scholarship.
Only if an athlete's goal is to be on the national team or
compete internationally does she seek the highest ranking.

Most of the girls competing on television or in the Olympics are Elites. Not many gymnasts attain this level; it takes
many hours of intense training and can be very expensive. An
athlete has to qualify to be an Elite by receiving certain scores
in special qualifying meets.

"Kim came to my gym when she was five years old and
gradually went through all the competitive levels until she
became an Elite gymnast,"[15] Bela said.

Even though Kim trained at Bela's gym, he did not coach
her personally until he felt she was good enough. Bela only
coached the top girls in his gym. The gymnasts learned the
skills while they were younger, then Bela would perfect them.
Kim was asked to join Bela's prestigious group in 1987 when
she was eleven years old, and she qualified to be an Elite the
next year when she was twelve.

Being in Bela's group was a difficult adjustment at the
beginning. Kim had a hard time understanding Bela's heavy
Romanian accent.

Kim described listening to Bela speak: "When we first
started . . . he sits there when he's talking to you, and you just
sit there and smile, 'I have no idea what you're saying to me,'
but you're like, 'Okay, I'll smile anyway.'"[16]

Although Bela and Martha spoke English to the gymnasts,
they spoke Romanian when they needed to talk privately.
However, one of Kim's teammates at Karolyi's gym, Betty
Okino, could understand Romanian since her mother was from
Romania.

"When I first came to the gym," Betty recalled, "they

didn't know that I could speak Romanian, and when they didn't want us to hear something, they'd speak Romanian."

Bela didn't understand how Betty knew what he and Martha were saying: "After awhile I figured that, 'Oh, wait a second.' Even before I start to step into the scene there were some indications. What was the matter? I said 'Golly, this kid can really read my mind, read my thoughts. What's going on?'"

"Somebody told them that I understood Romanian, so they stopped and they started speaking Hungarian, which I don't understand at all,"[17] Betty said with a chuckle.

Being in Bela's group meant a greater sacrifice of time and money. Parents would pay upwards of $3,000 a year for their children to train with the guru of gymnastics. That is, if they lived in the Houston area; if not, room and board were extra. In addition, there were the other expenses for leotards, hand grips, shoes, special braces to support ankle or wrist injuries, and travel expenses to competitions.

Kim described a typical day for herself and her teammates: "We go to the gym in the morning and we work out for a few hours. Then we go to school from 11:00 to 2:30." Kim attended Northland Christian School because it accommodated her training schedule. She only studied a few subjects, like geometry, biology, and Bible, because she did not attend school for the full day. Her favorite subject was "anything to do with math." Kim continued: "Then I come home, eat my dinner, take a nap, and go back about 4:30 and stay at the gym until about 8:00. Then I come home and do my homework."[18] It was a pretty demanding schedule, especially for someone so young.

Kim worked out roughly thirty-six hours a week. Why did she need to train so many hours a day? Simply, to be the best. There was only one chance in the competition to perform a routine, and the margin for error was so small that many repetitions of the same skills were required to make the gymnast more comfortable and improve her chances of hitting the skills.

According to Mary Lou, competitions provided a welcome break from the endless training. "When you get to a meet," she said, "it's a relief because you only have to do it once."[19]

Kim said that after all the long hours of practice, "I'm usually pretty confident going into competitions. Bela makes sure that we're prepared for every competition that we go into."[20]

Bela wanted the athletes to be prepared both mentally and physically before a competition. "We are strict and sturdy during the workout schedule and that's the only way to pass some limits," Bela reasoned. "We are talking about passing human limits of the human effort. So what other people would consider it's all a major sacrifice, no, that's a pride. They have the excitement of improving, of competing, in all these major satisfactions together, and really, really bring, say, a happy life. They are happy kids. . . . I wish most of the kids in the world could have just a little bit of the satisfaction what they are going through almost every day."[21]

Kim's mom, Clarice Zmeskal, saw how Kim's busy schedule and intense training affected her personality. "She's very disciplined," Clarice said, "she's very obeying. I guess you could say that she's different, I think, than my other two because of the way she's been trained at the gym. She's more disciplined in life."

From the beginning, Kim was the one who wanted to do gymnastics. She was not forced or bribed by her parents. This helped her understand Bela's role and respect his authority.

"It's within us," Kim said. "We're doing this gymnastics for ourselves. We're the ones who want to be the best and he's there to motivate us and push us and coach us and teach us what we're doing wrong."[23] This healthy attitude helped her to win favor with Bela and improved her gymnastics.

Kim greatly respected Bela's coaching style. "He's a really good motivator," she explained. "He always thinks of something new: new skills, new ways of training, new corrections. We're never doing it just perfect; there's always something that can be even better, and I think that's what helps us keep going. He has a good mind for gymnastics."

If Kim was having difficulty with a particular skill, Bela would think of new tactics to help her learn.

"If he tells you something that's wrong," Kim said, "and he knows it can be changed, and we try to change it a certain way, but that doesn't go, he always has an alternative way it can work."

Kim also practiced with a special Romanian dance teacher, Geza Pozsar.

"We have a choreographer who comes down from California every two weeks to work with us," Kim said. "We work a lot on our compulsories and optional dance."[22] Geza created the floor routines for Bela's best gymnasts.

Kim had an extraordinary ability to deal with pressure. Bela claimed that of the four thousand girls he had coached in Romania and the United States, none of them could match the competitive spirit that she possessed.

"She has an outstanding capability to pull herself together and perform consistently under pressure," Bela said. "You can see it on her face that she'll do it, no matter what."[24]

Kim's mom would sometimes worry about the constant stress that her daughter was under. "I don't think they'll ever realize how much pressure is on these kids," Clarice explained. "They put all the pressure on themselves for one thing: because they want to do well. And you see some kids can do it and some kids can't. A lot of kids I've seen in the gym can perform well in the gym. They can do it in the gym, but when they get to a meet they can't take the pressure."[25] Fortunately, her daughter was one of those whose routines were even better in the meet, which frustrated the ones who had been working just as hard but lacked the nerves of steel needed to pull it all together during competition.

Kim had lived in Houston since she was born, so she had not left her family to continue training at a high level. "I think I'm really lucky," Kim said gratefully. "I don't think I could move away from my parents and my family, 'cause they're a major part of my gymnastics, the way they support me."

Kim was the oldest of David and Clarice Zmeskal's three children. She had a sister, Melissa, who was three years younger and a football cheerleader. Her brother, Eric, who was seven years younger, liked to swim and play baseball. When Kim was not working out, she enjoyed spending time with her family or doing other hobbies, like swimming, collecting bottles, and putting together jigsaw puzzles.

Kim attributed her athletic ability to her father, David. "My dad was in pretty much everything," she said. "He's an all-around sports person. My mom didn't do too much." Kim's dad had attended the University of Texas and enjoyed watching the football team play on the weekend.

The Zmeskal's lived just minutes from the gym in a big, pretty house. David Zmeskal was a sales manager, and Clarice was a computer operator.

Kim's parents always supported their daughter in her gymnastics career and often watched her during practices.[26] However, they were not overbearing. They let Kim decide for herself how involved she would be in the sport.

Kim's first major meet as an Elite was the 1988 American Classic held in Scottsdale, Arizona, on May 19-21. Kim was proud to be a member of one of the most prestigious clubs in America, Karolyi's Gymnastics.

It was a new thing for Kim, having Bela at her side at meets. Before, he had always been with the older girls. Kim enjoyed participating in Bela's pre-meet rituals. One that everyone looked forward to was finding a lucky penny.

"There is no competition where I'm going to [that] I don't find a penny," Bela said. "Through the years I became very used to it, and also I became very comfortable with it. It gave me a little moral support. Yes, I'm lucky. Here is the lucky penny, we go for it." Bela cracked a smile and continued, "The lucky penny story became a big story among everybody I ever coached. We've always been really, really looking for those pennies before the competition because we consider it part of the little luck we have to carry with us into the competition."[27]

Twelve-year-old Kim competed in the junior division at the American Classic. She placed ninth with a total score of 45.50, doing well enough to advance to the U.S. Championships, the meet that ranks the gymnasts for the upcoming season.

Kim was virtually unknown at this point. Her name was even misspelled in *International Gymnast* magazine as "Kimberly Zmeska."[28]

A month after the American Classic, Kim competed in the United States Classic in Athens, Georgia. She did not do as well as she had hoped, scoring 45.25 total points and finishing seventeenth behind her teammates Amy Scherr (sixth), Erica Stokes (seventh), and Kelly Pitzen (eleventh).

The 1988 McDonald's U.S. Championships were held July 7-10 in Kim's hometown of Houston, Texas. With the homefield advantage, she improved from the last meet and scored 46.40 points. She placed eighth overall, which assured her of a spot on the junior national team.[29] Her older teammates—Phoebe Mills, Brandy Johnson, Chelle Stack, Rhonda

Faehn, and Kristie Phillips—were vying for a spot on the 1988 Olympic team. The 1988 U.S. Championships marked the first of two competitions that would be used to select the United States Olympic team.

A gymnast must be at least fourteen in the year of the Olympics in order to be eligible to compete in the Games. Kim looked forward to 1992 when it would be her turn. Maybe then she would be known only by her first name like her predecessors Olga, Nadia, and Mary Lou. Maybe then she would just be known as Kim.

Chapter 2

BEATING THE COMPETITION

After the 1988 Olympics in Seoul, South Korea, the United States' women's gymnastics team disbanded. One by one all of Bela's seasoned veterans packed up their belongings and left. Brandy Johnson, the best American finisher in Seoul, had come to Karolyi's gym just before the 1988 Olympics, but she left shortly after accomplishing her goal of making the Olympic team. She decided to train at her home gym in Altamonte Springs, Florida. Chelle Stack, the youngest 1988 Olympian, continued after the Olympics but not with Bela. The alternates, Rhonda Faehn and Kristie Phillips, retired and went home. Phoebe Mills, the 1988 Olympic bronze medalist on balance beam, hung on the longest but in the end succumbed to homesickness and a fatigue illness similar to mononucleosis called the Epstein-Barr virus. She competed in her final major international meet, the American Cup, on March 5, 1989. She then retired and moved back home to her family in Northfield,

Illinois.

After each Olympic Games, a changing of the guard in women's gymnastics occurred. The older ones retired and the younger ones prepared and gained experience for the next Olympics. The year 1989 was no exception to this rule. Kim and her teammates were nipping at the heels of the remaining 1988 Olympic team members, and one day an even younger generation would be pushing them.

Gymnastics is a difficult and demanding sport. Training six to eight hours a day, six days a week, can take its toll on athletes both mentally and physically. A gymnast rarely stays on top more than a couple of years.

Kim first burst onto the scene and into the spotlight on July 27, 1989 during the Junior Nationals at the United States Olympic Sports Festival in Oklahoma City, Oklahoma. There America saw the emergence of the "Karolyi six pack"—Kim, Hilary Grivich, Kelly Pitzen, Amy Scherr, Erica Stokes, and Amanda Uherek. Kim and her teammates were no longer in the background or the shadow of gymnasts like Phoebe Mills. Interestingly, Kim would be the only one of this group to make the Olympic team in 1992. Hilary Grivich suffered from a shoulder injury and finished ninth at the Olympic Trials, while the other four retired before 1992.

Only thirteen years old, Kim led the field after the compulsory portion of the competition. Compulsories are prescribed routines that must be performed by each athlete on an event to demonstrate technical competence. For example, every gymnast performs the same floor routine to the same music. Watching the compulsory competition can be very monotonous, especially when listening to the same music over and over, which is why the compulsories are rarely televised.

Next was the optional round of competition. In the optionals, each gymnast performs routines she has created

17

herself to showcase her abilities. Kim began optionals on one of her best events, the floor exercise. Although she liked all four of the gymnastics events, her favorite was the floor exercise. She thought it was fun.

"I feel like I can express my personality the best through this routine," Kim said. "Also, I've always loved to tumble and dance."[1]

Bela agreed that the floor exercise complemented Kim's personality. "Since she was little, she was always liking to be watched and admired," he said. "She was always a little showgirl."[2]

Although Kim was only four feet three inches tall, her size did not stop her from opening with a high full-twisting double pike somersault. She danced to her European-flavored music before the crowd at the Myriad Convention Center, finishing her second and third tumbling passes with solid landings.

Bela greeted her with a bear hug, saying, "That was a good one."

Even at a young age, Kim involved the audience in her routine. She kept her eyes off the floor mat and played to the crowd.

Moving to the vault, Kim performed a decent tucked Yurchenko full. Next, on the uneven bars, she had some trouble with her double pike flyaway dismount and fell. Despite this error, she remained in first place.

"I'd probably say [my weakest event is] my bars," Kim admitted. "That's always been my hardest event."[3]

The ESPN television announcer, Barry Tompkins, remarked about the uneven bar fall, "It has shown some of the other competitors that Kim Zmeskal is at least human."[4]

Going into the final event, Kim was leading another rising star, Shannon Miller from Edmond, Oklahoma, by thirty-five hundredths (0.35) of a point. Before her hometown crowd

Shannon went to the floor, while Kim headed to the treacherous balance beam, which can often make or break a gymnast in competition. Shannon started cleanly but landed her final tumbling pass, a double pike somersault, a little short and had to touch her hands to the mat. This dropped her to third place. Meanwhile, Kim executed a beautiful beam set, including a back handspring to two layouts and a gainer layout.

"While I'm performing, I try to stay focused on what I'm doing at that very moment,"[5] Kim said. She did not let the mistake on uneven bars affect her performance on beam. Her only error was a small step on the double back somersault dismount.

When she finished, Bela hugged her and kissed the top of her head, affectionately laughing, "All right little piggy."

Kim scored a 9.725 and became the Junior National Champion after leading throughout the competition.

"It's very exciting to follow in the footsteps of Phoebe, Kristie, and Mary Lou,"[6] Kim stated after the competition, which was her first major victory. Kim's strong performance also helped her team claim the gold.

In the event finals Kim won three more medals, bringing her total medal count to three gold (team, all-around, floor) and two silver (vault, beam).[7]

Looking back on that competition, Kim told *International Gymnast* editor Dwight Normile, "I remember being very optimistic about everything that was going on and just very excited to be an elite gymnast—it was only my second year—and for all of the positive things that happened that year with my whole team. It just made me really look forward to the next two years."[8]

Bela was equally thrilled. "These little ones are stronger than the seniors," he announced. "I'm proud of them. Probably I am getting the most excited and proud as I ever am . . .

we see childish mistakes, but they are children. It's kindergarten now, but this kindergarten is going to the Olympics in 1992—I promise you."[9]

* * *

Shortly before Thanksgiving, Kim won first place at the 1989 American Classic. She competed in the senior division and scored 76.74 points. The placements were calculated using 60 percent of the compulsory score and 40 percent of the optional score. Kim's solid effort qualified her to compete at the U.S. Championships in June.

Bela's kids dominated the field. They took three of the four top spots in the senior group and two of the top positions in the juniors.

Kim also won some meets in Europe near the end of 1989, including a victory with Lance Ringnald over thirteen other couples at the Swiss Cup Mixed Pairs competition. Kim was the youngest and the smallest athlete. She impressed the spectators with her handspring front with a half twist on vault and her floating double pike flyaway on bars. Other victories included the Arthur Gander Memorial in Montreux, Switzerland, where Kim received a 10 on floor exercise, and the City of Popes competition in Avignon, France. Winning these three international meets helped her name to become recognized outside the United States and increased her popularity among foreign audiences and judges.

Kim competed against the world's premier gymnasts in the Deutscher Turner Bund (DTB) Cup on December 1-3, 1989 in Stuttgart, Germany. The best Soviets were there: Natalia Laschenova and Natalia Kalinina. The Romanians did not compete because of the political turmoil in their country and the recent stunning defection of their most prized athlete, Nadia

Comaneci.

Kim did well against the tough field, placing fourth overall. The European audience really enjoyed her floor routine. Unfortunately, she stepped out of bounds, which lowered her score to a 9.70.

In the event finals, Kim placed third on vault and second on balance beam. Her teammate, Amy Scherr, also did well, coming in fifth overall and third on floor exercise.

Bela was overjoyed. "I'm so happy with these kids," he exclaimed. "It feels just like the old times with Nadia and the others. Winning is always nice and always great, but when you show up with unknowns and they win against these big names, it's just great!"[10]

After the holidays Kim traveled to Marietta, Georgia, for the Peachtree Classic held February 17-18, 1990. It looked as if Karolyi's team would easily win until Amy Scherr and Erica Stokes were injured during warm-ups, leaving Bela without a team at the last minute.

In the individual competition, Kim effortlessly won the junior division and all four event finals. In so doing, she captured the hearts of the capacity crowd at the Cobb County Civic Center. Hilary Grivich and Sammy Muhleman, also from Karolyi's, placed second and third, respectively. In addition, fellow teammate Betty Okino, a new member of the Karolyi clan from Elmhurst, Illinois, who had joined in November 1989, won the senior division, resulting in a clean sweep and total domination by Bela's little soldiers.

Kim was proud to be a member of Bela's talented entourage. "Well, he's different than any other coach I see when I'm at meets," Kim observed. "But basically, I don't know what it would be like somewhere else, because I've been here since I started. I watched when Mary Lou was working out, and Phoebe and Kristie." Kim knew how much success Bela's coaching had brought his former students, and she was hoping her story would turn out the same way.

Kim had enjoyed the opportunity to see many great gymnasts train with Bela over the years, but when asked to name her favorite, she answered, "It would have to be Mary Lou . . . she's great to watch."[11]

A few weeks after the Peachtree Classic, Kim entered the 1990 McDonald's American Cup in Fairfax, Virginia. This meet was significant because it showcased the best gymnasts from many different countries, such as the United States, the Soviet Union, China, and Romania. It was a very prestigious international competition. Former American Cup Champions included such names as Nadia Comaneci, Mary Lou Retton, Kristie Phillips, and Phoebe Mills. Interestingly, all of these gymnasts had been coached by Bela Karolyi.

Kim described her goals for the American Cup: "I wanted . . . to get more people to know who I am and to get the experience behind me."[12]

In the preliminary competition, only two gymnasts per country may advance to the finals the next day. Becoming one of the finalists is usually a difficult task since the best gymnasts from each country are vying for these spots. Brandy Johnson from Brown's Gymnastics in Florida (and former 1988 Olympian and pupil of Bela Karolyi) was the favorite and the defending American Cup Champion. She was currently the top gymnast from the United States. However, she failed to make it past the preliminaries, placing twenty-second due to illness and injury. This opened the door for Kim, who had placed third overall and was anxious to better her position in the finals.

The finals were on March 4 at George Mason University. All the competitors began together on vault and followed Olympic order: vault, uneven bars, balance beam, and floor exercise. Since only one event took place at a time, it was much easier to watch. In most competitions, when there are many gymnasts competing, all four events are performed simultaneously like a four-ring circus.

Before the meet began, Bela gave Kim his usual pep talk. He always seemed to know how to motivate his gymnasts.

"He's one of the best motivators I've ever seen," Mary Lou said of Bela. "He'll get you in a competition, and he'll start massaging your shoulders, and he's going, 'Can you do it? Yes, you can do it,' and he just puts this fire inside of you that just really gives you the confidence to say, 'Yeah, I can do it. If Bela thinks I can do it, I can do it.'"[13]

Kim performed an excellent full-twisting layout Yurchenko vault, complete with flared arms, an outstretched body, and a stuck landing, which was good for a 9.937 and the lead. Natalia Kalinina, the representative from the Soviet Union and Kim's main opponent, executed a difficult double-twisting Yurchenko but had to take a step for a 9.875.

The next event was bars. Natalia, usually a nervous competitor, did an outstanding routine but hopped on the crucial landing. Uneven bars was typically the apparatus on which Kim was the weakest and most inconsistent. She had fallen on bars in the preliminaries, but she hung on in the finals to enhance her lead. She did two nice release moves, a Jaeger and a Tkatchev (or reverse hecht), and a beautiful double pike flyaway. She scored a 9.887.

"I accomplished what I wanted, especially on the bars since in the preliminary day I had a mistake and fell off," Kim commented later about her performance. "You know, since I got back in there the second day and made it, I was really pleased."[14]

Kim performed a solid balance beam routine containing a back handspring to two layouts and a double tuck somersault dismount which kept her on top in the standings. Natalia was able to put her nerves aside and do a world class routine to tie Kim's mark of 9.825.

Floor was the final event. Kim nailed all three of her tumbling runs for a 9.95. The crowd at the Patriot Center particularly loved her three whip backs through to a double tuck somersault. Natalia could not overtake Kim no matter what she did. She fought hard anyway and finished the meet strong with a 9.925 on floor. Sandy Woolsey of the Desert Devils in Tempe, Arizona, was the other American competing in the finals, and she finished fourth.

Kim was truly amazing in her first international meet on home soil. She had the highest score on every event in the finals.

This was a shock for Kim. "I have to admit I'm surprised, but Bela said I could do it," she said happily. "He knows a lot about this meet and he makes you feel very confident."[15]

Bela was also very pleased: "I was just looking at little Kimbo, and I was so happy for her, seeing her as the new winner of the American Cup, because I know what victory is going to mean for her future."[16] Bela knew that Olympic champions had won this meet, and if history repeated itself, Kim had a bright future.

Natalia Kalinina said her loss was due to "unnecessary errors" and consequently "training will be very hard next week."[17] She spoke highly of Kim, saying, "I cannot forget Kim Zmeskal's performance on the floor exercise to the tune of a Russian dance. It was very artistic and beautiful. Her performance on the balance beam was also fine. In general, she is a very talented gymnast."[18]

Three days after the American Cup, the McDonald's International Mixed Pairs meet was held at Villanova University in Philadelphia. This competition is usually more relaxed and can be a lot of fun. It lets the gymnasts unwind from the stressful American Cup.

The format is also unique. Each female gymnast is paired with a male gymnast from the same country. However, there are exceptions; if a particular country only sends a male gymnast, for example, then he will be paired with a female gymnast from another country. Each pair may compete on only three apparatuses of their choice. Both scores are added together, and the pair with the highest combined total wins.

Kim was paired with Lance Ringnald of Gold Cup Gymnastics in Albuquerque, New Mexico.

Lance commented about his partner: "I thought, 'Well, here's Bela's new age of kids, the up and comers, and she's a great competitor, a little stud.' I thought, 'Gosh, this girl—she knows what she's doing.'"

Kim chose to begin on vault. At that time, if a female athlete wanted to vault, she had to do it in the first round. The men could vault in the second round. Kim's first vault was good, but she had a small hop on the landing and received a 9.875. Her second vault was even higher, although she still had to take a small step. The judges rewarded her with a 9.90, which was to be the highest score of the day among all the athletes.

Lance chose the high bar, which can be risky because of the number of release moves involved and the difficulty of sticking the dismount. He performed quite well, however, for a 9.55. The only problem he had was a hop on his complex dismount, a double-twisting double layout.

Generally, the men's scores tend to be lower than the women's because the value of their skills is less than the women's. For example, most of the women's routines have a starting value of a 10, whereas the men may have a starting value of only a 9.80. So even if the routine is performed perfectly, the highest score the male gymnast can receive is a

9.80.

A combined total of 19.45 placed Kim and Lance fifth.

Kelly Garrison, the captain of the 1988 Olympic team, asked Kim how she felt after the first round. "Well, I feel really confident," Kim replied. "The American Cup gave me a lot more confidence. I'm just going to have fun today with it."[19]

Sixteen-year-old Natalia Kalinina, the runner-up to Kim in the previous American Cup, also started on the vault, and performed a low full-twisting Yurchenko. She had to touch her hands to the mat, which is considered a fall and results in a loss of five tenths. Any fall on any piece of equipment is an automatic deduction of five tenths of a point. Natalia's second vault was much better. However, her Soviet partner, Alexander Kolivanov, made some errors in his parallel bars routine which dropped them out of the running.

The Romanians had sent their Junior National Champion, Lavinia Milosovici (who would later win the bronze medal in the all-around in Barcelona). She began with a solid full-twisting Yurchenko. This was the vault many gymnasts used because it was valued at a 10 and the Yurchenko (roundoff entry) made it easier for shorter gymnasts to get the power they needed to generate twisting in the post flight. Lavinia's partner also performed well, advancing them to the next round.

At the end of the first round, the international pair of Hilary Grivich from Karolyi's and Felix Aguilera of Cuba was in first place. The top eight couples advanced to the next round.

Kim chose floor exercise for the second rotation. Sixty-seven-pound Kim flipped, twisted, and danced a nearly flawless routine before a full capacity auditorium. The audience was delighted, clapping to the beat of her music. Her routine had been choreographed by Geza Pozsar, who had also created

Nadia's and Mary Lou's floor routines. Kim again received a 9.90.

Meanwhile, Lance prepared for the vault. He did a nice full-twisting layout Tsukahara with a small hop. The men are only allowed to do one vault, which puts extra pressure on them to hit it. They do not receive a second try like the women. Lance was given a 9.55, which put his team in second place behind the Chinese pair of Chen Cuiting and Li Ge.

Hilary Grivich over-rotated her first tumbling pass and had to step out of bounds, but her partner did well enough on the vault to advance them to the final round in third place. Only one pair from the United States could advance to the finals, but Hilary and Felix counted as an international pair, so they were able to advance.

Of the three couples allowed into the final round, Hilary was first up, and she chose the uneven bars. She did a very good routine with a stuck double back dismount. Her Cuban partner, however, fell on a release move on the high bar, which knocked them out of gold medal possibilities. The Chinese pair had the lead going into the last round, but Chen Cuiting fell off beam and dashed their hopes of winning.

After Chen's fall, Kim thought to herself, "That opens up the door for us. Now both of us just have to go and not make any major mistakes."[20]

The attention now focused on Kim and Lance. All they had to do to win the title was stay clean and not fall.

Kim elected to do beam. She was solid as a rock on the four-inch-wide piece of equipment, earning yet another 9.90.

It was up to nineteen-year-old Lance to clinch the victory. He chose the floor exercise. All he needed was a 9.35 to capture the gold.

Bela rushed over to Lance's side to watch and encourage him through his routine. Bela was as concerned about Lance's performance as he was about his own student's. He really wanted Kim and Lance to win.

Lance hit all his tumbling passes. After a brief conference to discuss the score, the judges gave Lance a 9.40, which was just barely enough to surpass China and win the competition.

Kelly Garrison again interviewed Kim and asked her how she felt to be the International Mixed Pairs Champion.

"Well," Kim said, "I knew going into the last rotation that we just had to hit, because the two pairs before us had made mistakes."[21]

Lance chimed in jokingly, "She just kept saying, 'Come on, buddy, pull through!' And all I had to say was 'All right, Kim! Thanks!'" Lance did not seem to mind that even though he weighed twice as much as Kim, she pulled most of the weight for the duo. "I like the format of the meet. I like it that a girl can help you out,"[22] he chuckled.

After captivating the American audiences, Kim flew across the Atlantic Ocean to challenge the best gymnasts in Europe. In the spring, she competed at the International of France in the beautiful city of Paris. She placed a surprisingly close second to Svetlana Boginskaya, the reigning 1989 World Champion. Svetlana struggled to beat Kim by only twenty-five thousandths (0.025) of a point. However, Kim opened many eyes with her gold medal-winning floor exercise routine in the event finals.

At the age of fourteen, Kim had already been to France, Germany, Holland, Spain, and Switzerland. It was important for European judges to know her, especially since the 1992 Olympics were to be held in Barcelona, Spain.

Although she went to many places in Europe, she spent most of her time in the hotel and the gym. She did not get many chances to sight-see or go shopping.

"We don't get to see too much,"[23] Kim admitted.

Next on Kim's busy schedule was the United States

Challenge, an elimination meet held in Las Vegas, Nevada. Kim won her first head-to-head battle easily by defeating her opponent, Jennifer Mercier, by over a point. She breezed by Jenny Ester, who had a couple of falls, to advance to the third and final round.

While watching the other matches, Kim could be seen wandering around the arena wearing a T-shirt with one of her favorite cartoon characters, Bart Simpson, on the front.

April Fool's Day marked the finals. Kim pulled away from the other two competitors, Stephanie Woods and Wendy Bruce, on the first event by scoring a perfect 10 on her vault. She racked up a 9.825 on both the uneven bars and the balance beam, charming the sparse crowd at the Cashman Field Center. Kim wrapped up her effortless victory by earning another perfect 10 on floor exercise.[24]

Taking a break from the rigors of competition, Kim participated in a tribute to Nadia Comaneci in Reno, Nevada. The purpose of the exhibition was to welcome Nadia to the United States and recognize her contribution to the sport that had made her famous. Nadia had just defected from Romania.

The show honored Nadia and Bela. It was a dramatic moment when the two were reunited for the first time as free people. Bela had not seen Nadia since the 1984 Olympics in Los Angeles, where they both had been surrounded by government officials.

There was a special place in Bela's heart for Nadia. "1976 Olympics is like a first love," he said, "the one after years and years and years you find yourself in a situation and say, 'Good Lord, I just created the best gymnast in the world.' I did have a great contribution to provide the first all-around Olympic Champion ever for the country. That was a unique moment, no doubt about it."

But after Nadia had achieved such great success, the

Romanian government had begun to interfere with Bela's gymnastics school. Bela had fought back, making waves with the country's top communist politicians.

In the 1980 Olympics in Moscow, Bela protested a mark given to Nadia after the judges suspiciously deliberated for forty minutes. The Russians gave her a lower score than she deserved, which placed her second in the all-around and allowed a relatively unknown Soviet to win. The Romanian people considered Bela a hero, but the government was furious that Bela would go against the Soviet Union and call them cheaters. The Romanian President, Nicolae Ceaușescu, took away a large amount of funding for Bela's team and also removed much of his power and influence. After being forced to go on a tour with Nadia in the United States in 1981, Bela, Martha, and Geza Pozsar decided to defect.

Nadia described how she felt when she first learned of Bela's defection: "I remember when he gave me the kind of impression that he doesn't like too much to go back home. I was like, 'Let me go and check his [hotel] room.' I was scared to put the key [in the lock] and open the door. I felt like my legs were cut. When I opened the door and moved the door a little, [there was] nothing in the room, so then I realized that Bela is not coming back, and then I started to cry. I told everybody else Bela is not coming back. It was—whew—such a moment."[25]

Now, finally, after so many years apart, these two famous Romanians were united again under different circumstances. Kim was able to witness the reunion and offer Nadia a rose to acknowledge her great contribution to gymnastics.

* * *

In May 1990, Kim and Alexander Kolivanov, the men's

American Cup Champion, were pictured together on the cover of the prestigious gymnastics magazine *International Gymnast* (*IG*). Kim had made the big time.

When asked if she read *IG*, Kim replied matter-of-factly, "Yeah, I do, of course."[26] She had seen her idol, Mary Lou, and many other distinguished Bela Karolyi protégées featured on the cover, and now it was her turn. Many little girls who received the magazine cut out the pictures of Kim and plastered them all over their bedroom walls, dreaming of what it would be like to walk in Kim Zmeskal's shoes. Several fans even wrote to *IG* begging for more photos of and stories about Kim. Their requests were granted in June 1990 when Kim again appeared on the cover, this time by herself.

When asked if she was ready to be a superstar, Kim shyly responded, "Yes, I'm ready. That's what goes with it if I do well."[27]

After all of her competitions and travels, Kim returned to the gym to train for the U.S. Championships. The meet was to be held in early June.

Since gymnastics is a sport in which there is not really an off-season, an athlete must train year-round. If the gymnast is not competing, she is learning new skills to add to her routines for the next season. After just one week of vacation, a gymnast's timing can be off noticeably and her skills can lose some of their sharpness.

As the U.S. Championships and the Goodwill Games drew near, Bela made practices tougher.

"He gets a little more strict, and we usually up the workout hours a little when it comes time for a bigger competition," Kim stated. "But basically, what helps a lot is that all of us at the gym have grown up around champions like Mary Lou. It helps to see how she was treated and how it could turn out for me."[28]

Bela held a meeting with his girls to explain the serious-
ness of the upcoming competitions. "We can no longer afford
to be even the slightest bit lazy," he began. "You must be
willing to put in sturdy and solid performances day after day
based on your individual and unique capabilities—do not copy
each other. You must pay attention and focus on your own
goals. There will be no individual attention paid to those who
waste time. You know your own capabilities and I expect you
to perform at your highest level. Lowering your standards will
lower the quality of your performances, and I know you do not
want that. No more compromising."[29] Kim and her teammates
were motivated.

Kim was willing to increase her hours in the gym.
Luckily, she lived close to the gym, as did Bela. Karolyi's
gym was on the north side of Houston in a calm residential
area. A group of three one-story buildings, the gym could
easily have been mistaken for a warehouse.

The atmosphere during practice was serious. "We don't
usually talk very much in the gym," Kim said. "We have to
stay concentrated, and we're in the gym for so long. Most
people are just out playing around and stuff. It helps me in
school a lot, too, because it makes me more serious that I have
to do it."[30] Kim was a straight A student at Northland Christian
School, where she was a member of the National Honor
Society.

Training for almost seven hours each day was a big
sacrifice for a young girl, but Kim believed it was worth the
commitment.

"We are missing out on some things," Kim recognized, "but
there's a lot of things that people that aren't gymnasts are also
missing out on, like we get to go on a lot of trips, and we get
to meet a whole lot of people. It's just—I don't know how it
is, really, anymore, to be a normal person, but I like what I'm

doing. Otherwise, I wouldn't be doing it."[31]

Kim had a reputation for being sweet and friendly, although she was all business while practicing. She worked in silence and was often upset and frustrated with herself when a move was not going well. She was a perfectionist, like her dad, and stubborn—a trait her mom insisted she got from Bela. She was also overly-organized and compulsively neat.

"I'm not an average teenager," Kim explained. "I'm four feet five and seventy-one pounds. When I first came to school they were like, 'Are you sure she's in what grade you said she's in? She looks like she's in second grade.' I'm used to it now. I want to be tall enough to be able to wear the kind of clothes I want to. I have a hard time shopping."

On the other hand, there were some advantages to Kim's size. "Being small in gymnastics helps a lot. With a small body to carry around, it makes tricks a lot easier,"[32] she reasoned.

Kim followed a strict low-fat diet that excluded junk food like ice cream. She had to be concerned with what she ate because her short and powerful body type was more prone to gain weight than that of a taller, long-legged athlete. But Kim was not always so conscientious with her food intake; once in awhile she would indulge herself. She had a weakness for sweets.

"We probably should watch our weight a little more than we do," she confessed sheepishly. "During the week, we go down to this T.C.B.Y. that's really close, and they know us really well, so we eat a lot of frozen yogurt."

When Kim got a chance to relax, her favorite television programs were *The Cosby Show* and *Arsenio Hall*. She thought an appearance on *Arsenio* would be cool. She videotaped the NBC soap opera *Days Of Our Lives* and took a break from her fast-paced schedule to watch it between school and her evening workout in the gym. She admitted to having a secret ambition to act on the show some day.

Sunday was Kim's day off from practice. She liked to spend time with friends during the weekend.

"Erica Stokes and I seem to do the most stuff together," she said, "like during the weekends . . . plus, she lives two streets down from me. We go to the movies a lot and stay at each other's house, just like normal kids do."[33]

As the summer approached and the school year ended, Kim prepared to leave for the U.S. Championships where she would battle the toughest gymnasts in the United States. She had won the Junior Nationals in 1989 and was now looking to conquer the senior bracket on her first try.

Chapter 3

THE NATIONAL CHAMPION

The next big meet on Kim's agenda was the 1990 U.S. Championships held June 7-10 in Denver, Colorado. This competition would decide the ranking of the gymnasts for the coming year. The higher an athlete placed, the more opportunity she would have to compete at major international competitions of her choice.

The compulsories were a battle between the veteran, Brandy Johnson, and the youthful Kim. Brandy, the defending United States Champion, emerged as the leader at the end of the day by fifteen hundredths (0.15) of a point.

The next day, Brandy began the optionals on vault with a beautiful full-twisting layout Yurchenko. She had good height but had to take a small step, earning a 9.80. Brandy opted to do a different second vault, which is normally done only in event finals. She performed a nice handspring front pike with a half twist and again took a small step. This time, the judges awarded her a 9.85. The higher score of the two was used.

Meanwhile, Kim was getting ready for balance beam. Beam can be a tough event to start on; however, Kim was a steady beam worker and was very tough mentally in competition.

Bela gave her some advice to motivate her before she began. "Good physical, good action, strong, good polish, and sharp," he reminded her.

She nodded, took a deep breath, and then raised her arms to acknowledge the judges. Her tumbling on the four-foot-high apparatus was stable, but she had a slight wobble on her full turn and a little hop forward on the dismount. Kim knew she could have done better.

"It wasn't bad," Bela mumbled as she walked toward him. The judges flashed a 9.675, which greatly displeased Bela. He wondered how they could take over three tenths of a point on a slight bobble and a hop on the dismount.

He discussed this with his wife, Martha, growling, "This is not fair. I'm leaving the competition. We cannot compete in this condition."

Bela thought the United States' judging system needed a major overhaul. "[The] selection system of the U.S. is very flawed," he said. "The whole point is to put your best athletes on the floor, and judges are a part of that process. We need to open the judging system in this country to create opportunities for our former international athletes to be involved."[1] Bela wanted previous gymnasts who understood the sport—like Mary Lou Retton or Kathy Johnson—to have easy access to becoming a judge.

Martha helped to smooth things over with Bela. As always, she played the part of Bela's calm, silent partner.

"I think we complement each other; probably I'm more the balance," Martha explained. "Bela sometimes gets overexcited.

He and I always keep the balance and just push toward the consistency, the importance of everyday work and preparation."

Martha usually refused to give television interviews because she was shy. "It's not my favorite thing," she said about being interviewed. But inside the gym her shyness disappeared. She expected and demanded a lot from her pupils. Martha was an excellent balance beam coach.

"I really enjoy the job that I'm doing on the beam," she said. "And lots of my gymnasts did a great job on the beam."[2] Over the years, she had instructed such great beam workers as Nadia Comaneci, Ecaterina Szabo, Julianne McNamara, Kristie Phillips, and Phoebe Mills.

Martha succeeded in calming Bela, and Kim moved to her next event: floor exercise.

"Normal, smooth, strong," Bela told Kim before she began.

Her first tumbling pass, a full-twisting double pike somersault, was excellent, and her dance, as always, played to the crowd. Kim's middle tumbling run—three whip backs to a double tuck somersault—caused an explosive reaction from the audience at the Denver Coliseum.

The NBC television announcer, Joel Meyers, remarked, "Right now it's a minute-and-a-half love affair going on between Zmeskal and this crowd in Denver." Her final tumbling pass, a double tuck somersault, was solid, and she scored a 9.80.

Brandy headed to the uneven bars intending to keep her small lead. She decided to be conservative and remove one of her two release moves. However, she had some trouble and barely made her giant swing over the bar, arching her back to avoid a fall. Reflecting the errors, the judges gave her a 9.50. At the halfway point of the meet, Kim trailed by only five hundredths (0.05) of a point.

Brandy moved to the balance beam. She was quite shaky

with a few wobbles early in the routine. Suddenly, she fell on her two back handsprings to a layout, which proved to be the turning point of the meet. She finished her unsteady routine and was consoled by her coach, Kevin Brown. She received a dismal 9.325.

On the other side of the arena, Kim was warming up for vault.

"At first I wasn't aware that she had fallen," Kim remembered, "because we were still doing the thirty-second touch [warm-up] for vault, and I came back and Amy [Scherr] said to me, 'Did you see that?' and I was like, 'See what?'"

Amy told Kim about the fall. With new inspiration, Kim went on to stick her vault for a 9.975. It looked like the title would be hers if she could just stay on the uneven bars.

Bela helped to keep Kim focused by gently shaking her shoulders and saying, "Kimbo, keep your mind straight now. Be a tiger. One more to go." She nodded in agreement.

Her routine was good, but she had to take an extra swing after her Jaeger. This was only a small error, though. Kim was relieved that she had at least grabbed the bar, because just prior to her routine in the touch warm-up, she had fallen several times on her Jaeger. The judges flashed a 9.50, making her the new and youngest ever United States Champion.

After the meet, Kim recalled what was going through her mind during her last event: "Bela told me to just make sure that I grabbed the bar and not make a major fall, so that's what I did."

"Good job," Bela said, giving her a hug. He grabbed her by the shoulders and looked intently into her big blue eyes. "Do you want to be a hard worker? Do you want to work a little harder?" he asked.

Kim nodded and softly answered, "Yes."

Bela continued, "I know it's worth it. I promise you, it's

worth it. But I'm proud of you still."

Brandy's final event was the floor. Unfortunately, her problems persisted through this last routine. She bounced out of bounds on her first tumbling pass and then did a double tuck somersault for both her second and third passes—errors that result in deductions. She received a 9.475, which placed her third behind two of Bela's students, Kim and Betty Okino.

Kristi Krafft interviewed Kim after the meet. She asked Kim if she had expected to win.

"Well," Kim answered, "after compulsories I wasn't really sure, because I was a little behind Brandy and I wasn't sure if I was going to be able to pull up. But I did my best, and I did."[3]

Kim later described her future plans: "Right now I'm looking forward to competing at the Goodwill Games and next year's World Championships and then the Olympics in '92."[4] She continued, "When you win anything, it motivates you so much to do even better."

Bela had trained three of the top five competitors in the senior division as well as the junior division champion, Hilary Grivich.

"It's a grand slam," Bela exclaimed. "This is the first time."[5]

This competition marked the midway point between the 1988 and 1992 Olympics. Some 1988 Olympic team members, like Brandy Johnson and Chelle Stack, were still lingering with distant hopes of making a second Olympic team. These two former Karolyi athletes had participated in the U.S. Championships but under the direction of new coaches.

Bela realized what valuable experience it was for his young athletes to compete with and be challenged by the experienced veterans. "I'm asking you, which is easier: to come with something you already got and compete back and forth, or to go back and work really, really hard—gosh, to create a totally new generation?" he questioned. "I was the one that chose the hard way. And all of my life I've done it the same way: to go back and create a generation. And I believe now that people should be very, very happy to have this unique situation in the country when two great generations can meet each other, can create a competitive environment, a very strong challenging each other. And who is the winner? The overall program, the quality [of] the team."[6]

The event finals were held the day after the all-around final. Steady and consistent Kim won silver medals on uneven bars, balance beam, and floor exercise.

* * *

The U.S. Championships served as the trials for the Goodwill Games, which were held July 27-29, 1990. First held in Moscow in 1986, the Games took place every four years to promote good relations between the United States and the former Soviet Union. The location alternated between the two countries. The next Goodwill Games were to be held in St. Petersburg, Russia, in 1994.

The top four gymnasts in the optional round of the U.S. Championships qualified for the Games in Seattle, Washington. Three of the four—Kim, Betty Okino, and Amy Scherr—were from Karolyi's gym. Sandy Woolsey also qualified.

Bela was pleased with the team. "I think this is a very aggressive and efficient group," he stated confidently. "This group has a chance . . . and no matter who comes, these people are going to fight for every single hundredth of a tenth . . . you can expect a big surprise at these Goodwill Games, because these kids are gonna carry with them not just a hunger of the big performance but a pride of competing in this country, and the public is going to carry them on their wings."

Up until 5 p.m. the day before the meet, Kim's competition status was questionable. She had planned to compete at the U.S. Olympic Cup in Salt Lake City, Utah, just prior to the Goodwill Games, but a nagging wrist injury had prevented her.[7] She had been suffering from tendinitis in her left wrist and bursitis in her heel. The doctors had said she would not do any more damage if she competed in the Goodwill Games, but there would be a great deal of pain that she would have to mentally block out. She decided to take her chances and compete despite the pain.

The first day was the team competition. The United States was hoping to win a team medal of some sort, possibly gold.

"If we came away with a medal it would show the world that the United States is ready . . . to come back as a team, and that our younger girls are getting stronger," Kim declared. After a disappointing fourth at the 1989 World Championships (at which none of Bela's kids had competed), the United States was hoping to redeem itself in Seattle.

Kim qualified as the top gymnast for the United States, and the media was quick to match her against the Soviet Union's Svetlana Boginskaya. This was to be one of many battles between Kim and Svetlana, who was often called the "Goddess of Gymnastics."

These two gymnasts were very different. For example, Kim was four feet five inches tall, while Svetlana was five feet four inches. Kim's strength was power and quickness, while Svetlana showed grace and elegance.

For all the media hype, the battle was disappointingly short-lived this time. On her first event, the uneven bars, Svetlana lost her grip on the bar after her Tkatchev release move and fell. This error threatened her chances of competing in the all-around finals, since only the top two finishers from any country qualified for the finals.

Kim began on beam with a reverse planche—her trademark skill—followed by a solid back handspring to two layouts and a back handspring layout to one knee. Her roundoff double tuck dismount was stuck cold, earning her a 9.90 and a big hug from Bela.

For the first time ever in women's gymnastics, the United States had a slim lead over the Soviet Union after the first rotation. This was particularly remarkable considering that the U.S. had so far competed only on the beam, one of the most difficult apparatuses in gymnastics.

Kim moved her sore wrist in circles to keep it loose during breaks in the competition. Despite the pain, which someone unaware of her injury would never have noticed from her blank facial expressions, she performed nearly flawlessly.

"The doctor told me that it can't get any worse," Kim said of her injury. "It's not dangerous to go and compete. It will still have pain, but there's no risk really . . . it hurt a little bit, but once I got out there, it was the last thing I was thinking about."

Kim continued her momentum to the floor exercise. She hit all three of her tumbling passes and received a 9.937.

The Soviets found themselves in a difficult position at the beginning of the second rotation when their first gymnast up, Oksana Chusovitina, fell from the balance beam. However, the others were able to pick up the slack. Their anchor, Svetlana, equaled Kim's floor mark of 9.937.

The United States moved to the vault while the Soviet Union went to the floor exercise. The U.S. team performed adequately but ran into a technical problem. Betty Okino did her second vault before the judges lit the green light signaling her to begin. Although the light was red, Betty thought they had told her to go. This resulted in a zero on her second attempt. Luckily, Betty had received a 9.80 on her first vault, so that score was counted.

Kim did a good first vault but took a large step. The judges gave her a 9.875, but she knew she had the ability to do better.

Bela prepared her for the second vault. "You were a little too high on the first one," he said referring to her hand position on the vault. "Bigger extension, strong."

Kim took advantage of her second try and did an outstanding vault—so high it should have been nicknamed Air Zmeskal —for a 9.912. The 16,000 fans cheered wildly.

Kim said the audience in Seattle helped. "I really like the crowd. I think it's easier to compete when there is a whole bunch of people behind you,"[8] she grinned.

The Soviet Union was not to be outdone, however. They performed superbly on the floor exercise to pull ahead of the United States.

The U.S. team marched to its final event, the uneven bars, and the Soviet Union went to the vault. Kim did a great uneven bar set complete with a Jaeger, a Tkatchev, and a double pike dismount with a solid landing. The judges flashed a 9.912, which was good enough to place Kim first in the all-around during the team competition.

The United States finished second behind the Soviet Union. The Chinese team, which had defeated the U.S. in the 1989 World Championships, placed third. Placing second in the Goodwill Games helped boost the United States team's confidence in future international competitions.

"This was the best performance we ever had against the Soviets," exclaimed an overjoyed Bela. "We really gave them a serious run for their money. Our challenge will be to do it for the [1991] World Championships."[9]

Interestingly, the Romanians had only sent one gymnast,

Gina Gogean. The funds had not been available to send the entire team due to the political turmoil in their country. Kathy Johnson, the captain of the 1984 Olympic team, said it was rumored that the Romanian team members had gone to the airport packed and ready to leave for the Goodwill Games before learning the heartbreaking news that there was no money to send them. The Romanians would have been tough to beat: they had placed second behind the Soviet Union in the 1989 World Championships.

Bela, the former Romanian national coach, gave his views of the situation: "Financially, their country is in deep trouble, and when they have to pull back their athletes, not being able to support financially the trip, that's a very sad situation . . . the Romanians have been more proud than anything of their own athletes—Nadia and all the other kids who have been so famous—and they gave so much pride for those people. And if they came down to the point they cannot even send them out to compete, that's a sad, a very sad situation. And sure, I feel very bad about it."[10]

Kim was interviewed by Hannah Storm after the competition. Hannah asked her about the Soviets and their winning performance.

"You can't really think about the other performers," Kim replied, "because they're not going to have anything to do with your scores and you won't have anything to do with theirs."

When asked to name the event with which she was happiest, Kim smiled, "My bars, definitely. That's been my weakest event, and I just went in and I didn't have very much time to think about it since I came right from vault, and that's the one I was most happiest with."[11]

The all-around final was the following day, July 28. Since only two gymnasts per country may advance, Svetlana Boginskaya did not qualify because of her fall on the uneven bars.

However, the Soviet Union decided to take out Tatiana Lisenko, who had qualified to the all-around. Her coaches claimed she was injured and replaced her with Svetlana.

Bela grumbled, "Putting [Svetlana] back in is unfair for all the competitors here. [The Soviets] need to play by the rules just like everyone else."

The Soviets had been known to pull stunts like this in the past. In the 1985 World Championships in Montreal, Canada, they had replaced two gymnasts who had qualified to the all-around final with Oksana Omelianchik and Elena Shushunova. Both went on to tie for the all-around title. The same situation was to occur in the 1992 Olympics when Tatiana Gutsu fell on balance beam in the team competition but was able to compete in the all-around final after the Soviets substituted her for Roza Galieva, who supposedly injured her knee.

People speculated that the reason the Soviets did this was to ensure their best gymnasts were in the all-around final regardless of how they had performed the day prior. The substitutions were a controversial topic, and many people disagreed with the ethics of the Soviet Union. Still, the Soviets remained on top and produced some of the world's finest gymnasts.

Kim led the field after the team competition, but the scores did not carry over to the all-around final. Everyone started with a clean slate. Sometimes that meant a second chance. Sometimes it meant an athlete had to prove herself all over again.

Unfortunately for Kim, she fell ten minutes into the all-around final on her first event, the uneven bars, which dashed her hopes of winning a gold medal.

Kim said about the mistake on her Jaeger, "I just let go of the bar too early."[12] She was clearly disappointed with the fall. "I was just wishing that I would have done the same bar routine

I did yesterday, but, of course, everyone wants to do the best routine all the time, and I can't always have it."[13]

Betty Okino, the other American to qualify, banged her foot on the low bar following her Tkatchev release move. The Americans were not off to a good start.

Svetlana also began on uneven bars, the same event with which she had had trouble in the previous day's team competition. While she had no major errors, her set was a conservative one with only one release move, a Tkatchev. Most gymnasts at her level would have performed two.

In the second rotation, Svetlana did a nice beam routine with a slight wobble on her tumbling series. Kim came back after her fall on the previous event with a solid balance beam routine for a 9.862.

Svetlana next competed on the floor. Her exotic style was somewhat different from that of the other athletes. She hit all her tumbling passes on floor to maintain her lead.

Kim tried to stay focused and finish strong on her remaining events. "After the fall I knew I had to keep my momentum going," she recalled. "I knew I still had the rest of the competition to compete."[14]

After a long pause because of judging discrepancies over the previous gymnast, Kim was allowed to begin. Her routine was good, especially for someone with a sore wrist and heel. However, her famous middle pass of three whip backs to a double tuck somersault was not as strong as usual; it looked like she had some difficulty keeping the momentum going on her whip backs, but she covered nicely. She sparked the interest of the sold-out audience, and they clapped loudly to the beat of her music.

"I heard them," Kim said. "The crowd helped a lot."[15] She scored a 9.95.

Betty Okino finished the competition with a solid vault to

place fourth in her first major international competition. Kim also ended on vault. Her first vault was lower than normal, possibly because of her injury. It is much harder to get a good push off the vault for height in the post-flight with an injured wrist.

Kim looked disappointed as she walked toward Bela for some advice. He told her some key words to remember: "Stronger, faster, faster off, down on the ground. Okay?"

Kim nodded and hurried back to do the second vault. The judges flashed a 9.787 for her first attempt and lit the green light signaling her to try again. Kim ran down the runway determined to improve. She exploded off the springboard, flew through the air effortlessly, and landed without budging, as if she had glue on the bottoms of her feet.

Kim smiled and ran toward Bela, who welcomed her with open arms saying, "A little makeup for all the other ones, huh?" She scored a 9.925 and finished sixth in the all-around.

Natalia Kalinina won the gold in the all-around, while Svetlana had to settle for the silver. Henrietta Onodi of Hungary got the bronze.

Bela was confident that Kim would challenge the Soviets even more in the future. "The competition will go on with Kim and Kalinina," Bela predicted. "I was very pleased with the team competition last night. We are still happy about tonight. This creates more hunger and is a good lesson for everyone that we've got to work and fight for it."[16]

Kim recalled how she felt after the first two days of the Goodwill Games: "I thought the first day went perfectly. I was just so happy about that, because two days before the competition I wasn't sure if I was going to compete. But the next day taught me a lesson that I have to have more consistent workouts and go in the gym with a much better attitude all the time. That's just what happened with my bar routine. I hadn't been consistent enough."

Kim used this experience to motivate herself. Although injuries had prevented her from training as hard as she had wanted before the meet, she had still beaten some of the best gymnasts in the world during the team competition. That showed what Kim was capable of doing.

"That just gives me more confidence in wanting to work harder, and makes me think I can be the best if I work at it,"[17] Kim said with a sparkle in her eye.

Svetlana, the voice of experience, commented about Kim's fall, "You don't go through a sport without some falls. This will serve to her advantage eventually."[18]

The next day was the event finals. Competing three days in a row can be very draining on the athletes. The event finals are often not as exciting, since most of the pressure is in the all-around competition. Typically, there are more falls in the event finals, and the gymnasts only compete in the events to which they qualify.

The top eight finishers on each event in the team competition vie for gold in the event finals. All the same rules apply as in the team and all-around competitions, except in event finals the gymnasts must perform two different vaults, and the scores are averaged instead of taking the best of the two scores.

Kim qualified to all four event finals, but she elected not to compete on vault due to her sore wrist. She was planning to do a better uneven bar routine this time.

"I just mainly wanna get my confidence back and hit the routine,"[19] Kim stated.

She did an excellent bar routine. She hit all of her release moves (which had given her trouble in the all-around competition) and stuck the dismount for a 9.90. Kim placed third behind Natalia Kalinina and Zhang Xia of China, who tied for the gold.

"I'm really happy," Kim said with relief. "I'm glad I could come back after yesterday's disappointment."[20]

Kim did a nearly flawless balance beam routine, complete with a stuck dismount, for a 9.90 and fourth place. Unfortunately, she was one of the first gymnasts to compete, and the scores tend to be lower for the first gymnasts in order to leave room for higher scores if a later athlete does better.

Kim hoped to win a medal in floor event finals. "If I medal in these games and in floor exercise, it will mean a lot to me, because this is a very major competition for me, and the whole world's watching,"[21] she said with a smile.

She saved her best routine of the competition for last. The large crowd at the Tacoma Dome loved her playful dance and perky tumbling.

After her superb floor routine, Bela greeted her by saying, "That's beautiful. You did good."

Kim scored a 9.912 and took the bronze behind the familiar Soviet duo of Svetlana Boginskaya and Natalia Kalinina, who tied for the gold.

Kim described to *International Gymnast* editor Dwight Normile the experience of her first major battle against the Soviets: "That was very exciting for me because it was the first really big competition for me, and also my teammates, because we had never been in a World Championships or the Olympics or anything. And to be so close to the Soviets really gave us a lot of confidence, especially myself, and competing internationally and not being afraid of the competition, being able to go in and actually think that I could pull something off in the all-around standings. It was a really good experience for me, especially since it was in the United States."[22]

Bela was asked by Hannah Storm after the 1990 Goodwill Games how the United States did overall. He replied, "It was a very stormy weekend for us with all the ups and downs, but

I'm very, very glad. Finally, we see some young really up-and-coming generation on the podium and standing tall and strong, and I hope that's just the beginning of many, many victories from now on."

Hannah wondered how good the Americans were in relation to the Soviets. Bela responded, "Probably the best statement is, if we are looking back last year, these kids were only juniors on our Olympic Sports Festival competing and now up on the international podium. Even not [winning] the gold but they are right, right next to that, and that's very important for us."

When asked how this performance would position the U.S. team for the World Championships in Indianapolis in 1991, Bela said, "I am very positive. We are in a very good shape. We got a lot of respect, and now on the international so-called 'politics'—what the judges are representing—we gained a lot of respect, a lot of recognition during this meet."[23]

Alexander Alexandrov, head coach of the Soviet women's team, was not impressed by the United States and said flatly, "As for our main competitors, I would still single out the Chinese team, not the U.S., whom we beat by only 0.275 in the team competition due to breaks on bars. The head coach of the Americans, Bela Karolyi, has been talking a lot about how his team will beat the Soviet team at the next World Championships in Indianapolis in 1991. But in our view, his girls still don't have any particular chance at that. But the Chinese are progressing very quickly."[24] (Interestingly, Alexander Alexandrov would eventually leave his homeland and work for Bela in Houston in 1994.)

After the Goodwill Games, the Soviets stayed in the United States for an exhibition in Portland, Oregon. Shortly thereafter, the United States versus the Soviet Union meet was held on August 4 at San Jose State University in California.

The National Champion

The reigning 1989 World Champion, Svetlana Boginskaya, elected not to compete. Cathy Rigby-McCoy said the Soviet coaches had decided to use the younger gymnasts so that they could gain more experience for the 1992 Olympics. Besides, the Soviets had been traveling in the United States for the past twenty days, and some of the athletes needed a break.

Also not competing was the defending USA versus USSR Champion, Brandy Johnson. Kim had snatched the American Cup title and the United States Champion title away from Brandy Johnson; maybe this third title would be a charm.

The Soviet Union began on vault, while the United States went to the uneven bars. Kim started the competition on the right foot by scoring a 9.95 on bars, though she had a little trouble keeping the momentum going after each release move. She was in a great position to move up in the standings after completing her weakest of the four apparatuses and maintaining second place behind the Soviet, Oksana Chusovitina. Betty Okino also score a 9.95 on bars to tie with Kim.

Kim next moved to the balance beam, which was normally a very strong event for her. She hit all of her skills and again received a 9.95, but this time the score was good enough to put her in the lead. Natalia Kalinina, the recent Goodwill Games winner, lost her concentration and consequently had several breaks on uneven bars. The errors cost her a chance at the all-around title, as the judges gave her a disappointing 9.40.

Meanwhile, the young United States athletes were challenging for the team title on floor exercise. Hilary Grivich turned in a solid routine, as did Betty Okino for a 9.95. Kim was the United States' anchor (last to compete) for the third rotation. She began with a perfect full-twisting double tuck somersault and immediately involved the intimate crowd at the Activity Center in her routine. Kim nailed her three whip backs and her final tumbling pass to maintain her lead with a score of 9.975.

Even though Kim was at the top of the standings, she still saw room for improvement. "When I see the Soviets and some of the other Americans, too, I'd like to have more flexibility, which I'm working on and which has improved greatly over the years," she said. "When I first started, I could barely do anything." With admiration for her Eastern counterparts, Kim added, "But I really like how the Soviets dance. And Betty Okino, I really like her dance, too."[25]

Kim moved to her last event: the vault. She was still bothered by her sore left wrist that had tendinitis left over from the Goodwill Games. She used a special wrist brace that helped to take some of the pressure off but still allowed her to compete to her full potential.

Her first vault was very high, and she had to take a small hop.

Bela told her not to slow down before she hit the board, and added intensely, "Let's try the second one: stronger, more speed."

Kim needed a 9.825 to beat Oksana Chusovitina for the all-around title. She got much more than that as she soared through the air and landed without moving her feet for a perfect 10.

"I'm proud of you!" Bela announced joyously. "Good job!" He then told her to wave to the crowd, which brought more cheers and a standing ovation.

Kim described what she was thinking during her final event: "I don't keep up with the scores very much, but I just knew I could do the vault and went and I did it as well as I could."[26]

Kim set a new meet record with her all-around score of 39.875. As expected, the Soviet Union won the team competition, but the United States challenged them for the title and proved they would be a team to reckon with in 1992.

Surprisingly, Tatiana Lisenko, whom the Soviets had claimed was injured during the all-around final of the Goodwill Games allowing Svetlana to take her place, must have healed quickly to compete and finish fifth in this competition a week later. She did not score under a 9.80.

Nadia Comaneci praised Kim's performance, exclaiming, "She was really good. I love her. She made a mistake at the Goodwill Games, but now I don't think that she will do any mistakes from now. She's a great gymnast, and I think that she will become a champion."[27]

This meet marked the end of the competitive season. The gymnasts would take a small break, lasting a week or two, and then return to the gym to learn new skills for the new season which began for the most part in the early winter and lasted through the end of the summer.

Bart Conner, the 1984 Olympic gold medalist, asked Kim what she was going to do on her upcoming vacation. Kim replied, "Well, mainly just rest my arm and my leg and hope that it's better when I come back."[28]

Since the hard competitions were finished for the year and Kim needed to rest her aching body, she had some free time to autograph fan mail. Kim seemed to like her new fame and did not mind what accompanied it.

She smiled and said, "I've got a stack of letters from people I have to write back to. I'm making sure I'm writing everyone who writes me at least once."

Kim tried to keep all the attention she was receiving in perspective. "It's really weird," she said of her recent popularity. "I remember I would be so nervous just to go up and say hi to Mary Lou or Julianne or Phoebe, and now it's like that's how people are treating me. It's really strange. I'm trying to stay as normal as I can. I don't know; I'm trying not to change as a person too much."

KIM ZMESKAL

Kim elected not to compete in the 1990 World Cup in Brussels, Belgium, in October, because she wanted to rest the parts of her body with persisting injuries, like her sore wrist. Despite the aches and pains, she managed to experiment in the off-season with a couple of new skills.

"My routines are pretty much the same right now," Kim said. "We're working on a few tumbling passes, and we're not sure which ones we'll stick in."[29]

Kim was training a double layout somersault, which was one of the most difficult tumbling runs performed. She was also hoping to be able to end her floor routine with a full-twisting double pike somersault.

In November 1990, Kim participated in the Revco Gymnastics Tour of Champions along with Mary Lou Retton and Betty Okino. The tour went through several East Coast cities.

The United States Olympic Committee announced that Kim was the 1990 Female Athlete of the Year in gymnastics, and she placed seventh overall in SportsWoman balloting. Kim had won five major international and national tournaments in 1990. At the United States Gymnastics Federation (USGF) Congress banquet in New Orleans she was elected Female Athlete of the Year and Bela was honored as Women's Coach of the Year. Tiny Kim, who was just fourteen, charmed the audience, and they chuckled during her acceptance speech when she spoke about ". . . people you've been with since you were little." Kim was also one of the ten athletes nominated for the 1990 Amateur Athletic Union's (AAU) Sullivan Award, the highest honor in U.S. amateur athletics. This "Oscar" of sports awards was established in 1930 in honor of James E. Sullivan, the founder and former president of the AAU. In addition, Kim was chosen from more than one hundred top young athletes as the recipient of the Women's Sports Foundation's 1990 Up & Coming Award.[30]

Kim appeared on a large colorful poster that was accompanied by a lengthy interview in the December 1990 issue of *International Gymnast* magazine. The poster captured Kim holding her backbreaking reverse planche on balance beam in the United States' red leotard with white and blue stripes on the sleeves.

1990 had been a very successful year for Kim, but the Olympics were still a year and a half away. Kim wondered if she could keep her winning streak going that long.

"It sorta scared me that I was winning . . . and I was like, 'How can you keep going like this?'" Kim mused. "It scared me for a little while, but then I thought, 'Well, if I'm ahead right now and keep working as hard as the people behind me, I could stay like that.'"[31]

It is hard to remain on top for more than a year or two because there are always younger, talented gymnasts with which to contend. As the gymnast gets older, taller, heavier, and more bumps and bruises, the sport does not seem as easy as it once was. Also, the daily grind of practicing eight hours a day, six days a week, becomes more exhausting with age.

Kim had established herself as the one to beat. But could she keep her winning streak going?

Chapter 4

PROBLEMS WITH BELA

Kim began the new competitive season with a trip to Europe to gain some international experience. She journeyed to Barcelona, Spain—the host of the upcoming Olympic Games—to get a feel for the place where she hoped to strike gold in 1992.

The Joaquim Blume Memorial competition was held on December 1, 1990 in the future Olympic venue, the Palau Sant Jordi. Kim placed a disappointing sixth in the all-around behind Betty Okino. Svetlana Boginskaya won the meet and hoped she would be able to duplicate her first place finish the next time she competed in the building at the 1992 Olympics. On the individual apparatuses, Kim placed ninth on vault, thirteenth on bars, third on beam, and sixth on floor. She was not thrilled with her results.

At the Arthur Gander Memorial held in Chiasso, Switzerland, Kim improved her performance and won a bronze medal in the all-around with 39.10 total points. Betty won the silver and narrowly defeated Kim with 39.275 points.

Kim and Betty next traveled across the Swiss border to the neighboring country of Germany for the prestigious DTB Cup on December 7-8 in Stuttgart. Unfortunately, Kim was first up on vault and consequently received only a 9.887. Then the uneven bars collapsed, adding a twenty minute delay. But that did not faze Kim. She was solid on the event for a 9.75. However, she was a little shaky on beam for a 9.80. Kim's floor was a highlight for the audience at the Martin Schleyer Halle, and she earned a 9.912. Kim bettered her all-around mark from the previous meet, scoring a 39.349, but with the tough competitive field she only placed fifth. Betty came in second.

After the meet, Kim's spirits were low. She had not done very well. Svetlana Boginskaya, in a kind gesture, tried to comfort her.

"I had just come back from a wrist injury and so I didn't have a whole lot of time to prepare for the meet, and I didn't do as well as I would have liked to," Kim remembered. "I was about to start crying, because I was upset with how I did, and she came up to me and said, 'Don't cry, Kim.' And I like almost burst out, because when someone tells you not to cry, of course, it makes it worse. But that really meant a lot to me to hear that from her."[1]

Kim qualified for the event finals on three apparatuses, but Bela decided not to let her compete on vault. She placed a dismal fourth on beam and fifth on floor.

Once the DTB Cup concluded, Kim packed her bags and traveled to yet another European city: Beaucaire, France, for her final meet before Christmas. Her whirlwind tour of Western Europe was almost complete.

With her mind set on turning in a solid performance before

leaving, she improved greatly from the last meet and came in second overall with 78.25 points (compulsories and optionals combined) in the Recontre Beaucaire competition. Again, she was behind Betty Okino in the standings.

Surprisingly, after the compulsories, the United States team had captured the lead from Romania. The Romanians were very displeased. It was rumored that the Romanian coaches forced the girls to do an extra long workout a few hours before the optional round was to begin. Their country was in political turmoil, and they were desperate to win. Their strategy worked, because the Romanians surpassed the Americans slightly in the optionals to take home the team gold that they wanted so badly. In the event finals, Kim finished first on the floor exercise and third on balance beam.[2]

After an exhausting several weeks of traveling and competing, Kim returned home for the holidays but did not take any time off, because she had to prepare for the 1991 American Cup. Bela usually let his gymnasts take their vacation for a week or two in October instead of December. It was important to train at this time because many important meets were ahead. Spending the holidays in the gym was especially hard on the girls whose families were far away. Luckily for Kim, her family lived in Houston.

Shortly after ringing in the new year, Kim entered the Alamo City Invitational on February 8-10, 1991 as a warm-up for the American Cup. Bela took two teams of five gymnasts to San Antonio. His first string—Kim, Betty Okino, Kerri Strug, Hilary Grivich, and Chelle Stack (who had left Bela awhile ago and then returned)—easily won the team competition. Kim beat Betty by one tenth in the all-around and went on to win both beam and floor finals. The victory was a great birthday present for Kim, since she turned fifteen a few days prior to the competition.

Kim's gold medal-winning floor routine was created six days prior to the meet. The music she selected was the familiar tune of *"In the Mood."* The piece was arranged by Barry Nease of Floor Express Music in Frisco, Colorado, and the choreography was again done by Geza Pozsar.

Geza had been a classical ballet dancer for Romania before joining Bela's staff in 1974. Of all the great routines he had created, his favorite was this one he made up for Kim. This was quite a compliment of her since Geza did many, many routines for the finest and most talented gymnasts in the world.

A week after the Alamo City Invitational, Kim flew to Columbus, Ohio, despite a minor snow storm, for the 1991 Red Roof Inns Buckeye Classic. Fifteen hundred gymnasts of all ages competed. In the all-around competition, Kim fell on her relatively new release move on bars, a Gienger. This replaced her Jaeger, a skill that had sometimes caused problems for her in competition. The error dropped her to fourth place. Betty also fell on bars, but she placed third, slightly ahead of Kim.

Bela's kids were expected to win, and they did not disappoint anyone. Despite the falls, they won the team competition by almost four points. One thing was evident: Bela's girls were in much better shape than any other team because of the number of hours they had spent in the gym. They worked as a group. They were very organized, kept busy, and followed instructions. For example, during the warm-up, one person would tumble and stay in the corner after she was finished to help keep the next tumbler from falling off the floor if she made a mistake.[3] The athletes from other gyms could not help but notice and gawk curiously at the precision and accuracy of Bela's blue-and-white-striped army.

Kim once again packed her bags and headed south to Florida for warmth, sunshine, and the 1991 McDonald's American Cup. For the first time ever, the American Cup would reward the gymnasts' efforts by giving prize money. The first place all-around winner would take home $5,000, second place would receive $3,000, and third prize would be $2,000. In addition, each event winner in the preliminaries would receive $1,000. The only drawback was if the athlete accepted the money, she would no longer be eligible for NCAA collegiate competition. Also, a trust fund would have to be set up immediately following the meet, and if a gymnast failed to comply, she might not be able to compete in future competitions, including the Olympics.

Fifteen-year-old Kim entered the meet as the defending champion. In the preliminary round, she placed first ahead of teammate Betty Okino. Betty had beaten Kim at several meets in Europe a few months earlier, and the rivalry between the two promised an interesting competition in the finals.

Even though the two were close friends, Betty did not treat Kim any different from the other athletes in a meet. Betty described how she related to Kim in regard to gymnastics: "We have the same goal, we're working for the same thing, we're together all the time. When we're competing, we're competitors, we're teammates. You don't really think, 'Okay, there's my best friend.' She's just another competitor."[4]

The United States captured first through seventh place in the preliminaries, but only the top two finishers from the U.S. were allowed to move on to the finals the next day. Bela had four of the top seven athletes: Kim, Betty, Kerri Strug, and Chelle Stack.

The finals were held on February 23, 1991 in Orlando. A total of eight female gymnasts competed in the final round.

The first event for all the athletes was vault. Kim posted a 491 on the scoreboard at the end of the vault runway, which let the judges know what vault she would be attempting. She performed the same vault she had done in last year's competition: a full-twisting layout Yurchenko. She opened into a nice arched position and jetted her arms out—leather braces on both wrists—to show how early her four-foot five-inch frame completed the twist. The judges gave her a 9.925. However, the vault was not good enough to surpass Betty, who scored a perfect 10 with the same vault and established herself as the one to beat early in the competition.

Betty sailed through an outstanding uneven bar routine for a 9.90. Kim answered with a good routine of her own, taking only the slightest hop on the dismount for a 9.85. Still, she trailed Betty by 0.125 with two events to go.

Betty went before Kim on balance beam, giving Kim the opportunity to see what she had to beat. Betty executed a beautiful beam set; her long legs and arms definitely worked to her advantage. She hit a back handspring to two layouts, a very difficult double turn, a straddle planche, and two back handsprings to a double back dismount. Her only error was a small step on the landing.

Bela gave her a big hug, saying, "That was a good one. All right, good job." She scored a 9.937 to further her lead.

Kim needed a great performance to close the gap between her and Betty, but even a 10 would not put her in the lead. If Kim was going to win this competition, she needed near-perfect performances on both balance beam and floor exercise.

Kim began her beam routine with a nice mount followed by a reverse planche and her acrobatic-gymnastics (acro-gym) series, front handspring to a split jump.

Each gymnast must have a tumbling series of two elements or more, a leap series, an acro-gym series, and a full turn incorporated into her balance beam routine. She must also have a certain number of difficult skills, which are rated A (easiest) through D (most difficult). (After the 1992 Olympics, an E became the most difficult skill.)

Kim prepared for her tumbling series, back handspring to two layouts—the same one Betty and most gymnasts of that level performed—and nailed it without a bobble. Kim continued with a solid full turn and good leaps. However, on her new element, a back tuck swing down, she missed one of her hands as she grasped the beam to swing down, which caused her to lean to one side. She knew the judges would have to take a small deduction for that.

All that was left was the dismount. She had good height but had to take a hop on the landing.

Kim saluted the judges and walked toward Bela, disappointment showing on her face.

"My hand was off to the side," Kim complained to Bela regarding the mistake. He mumbled unhappily as the slight errors were reflected in the 9.787 score.

The final event, floor exercise, was always a crowd-pleaser. Kim and Betty were a sharp contrast on this apparatus. Kim was bubbly and aggressive, her main asset her tumbling ability, while Betty was graceful and soft, her dance background accenting her elegance.

One thing was sure: Bela could not lose tonight. One of his gymnasts would capture the gold. In order for Kim to win, Betty would most likely need to have an error.

Julianne McNamara, the NBC television announcer and 1984 Olympic gold medalist, commented that Betty had experienced difficulty with her opening tumbling run in warmups and had also been suffering from the flu virus for the past several weeks. It is difficult to perform on floor with a cold or other sickness because of the endurance and strength involved.

Betty began her classy routine to *"Jealousy"* with a high full-twisting double tuck somersault, and she was able to stay in bounds, despite her problems in warm-ups. She also executed a nice triple turn which was extremely difficult and would merit bonus points from the judges. Betty finished her dramatic routine with a solid double tuck somersault, and the crowd leaped to its feet to support her.

Bela hugged the new American Cup Champion, saying, "I'm proud of you! That's how you are supposed to do it. Good job." The judges announced a 9.95 which put her all-around score out of reach. Betty also set a new all-around record that had previously been held by Nadia Comaneci, the 1976 Olympic Champion. All Kim could do was fight for second place.

Bela walked over to Kim and encouraged, "Come on Kimbo, this is going to be a 10, huh?" He patted her on the back before she stepped onto the floor mat.

She struck a new beginning pose to go along with her three-week-old floor routine. The crowd immediately got involved as seventy-two-pound Kim dazzled them with her explosive first tumbling pass, a full-twisting double pike somersault. The audience at the Orlando Arena cheered and clapped while she effortlessly nailed all her tumbling passes. When she finished, the mesmerized spectators again jumped to their feet to endorse another fine performance. The judges liked it as well; they gave her a 10. This was Kim's third 10 on the floor exercise and fifth 10 of her career.

Despite her second place finish, Kim was pleased with her perfect score. "To finish like that makes up for a lot of it,"[5] she said.

Kim earned a big hug from Martha. "That was a good one," Bela said, giving her a hug as well. As they parted, Bela's wireless microphone used for television got caught in Kim's hair. She struggled to get free but could not, so Bela had to yank it out of her hair, which proved to be quite painful.

Bob Neumeier rushed over to interview Kim after her spectacular floor routine. He congratulated her on the 10, and she grinned and said, "Thank you. I've been waiting for this last event. This day didn't go exactly how I wanted it to, but I'm really happy to end like this."

Bob asked if she was happy for Betty. "Yeah," Kim replied, "I'm really happy for Betty. She's been trying really hard in the gym and it's really close between us a lot."

The final standings were Betty first, Kim second, and Ludmilla Stobvtchataya, a Soviet, third. Betty took home $7,000 in prize money (first all-around, vault, bars), and Kim received $5,000 (second all-around, beam, floor).

The American Cup demonstrated how Kim and Betty used their friendship to their advantage. On one hand they were like sisters, but on the other they were rivals.

"I think we push each other to do better in the workouts and in competition," Kim remarked. "We know each other, and we're such good friends outside of the gym that it helps us."

"Every now and then we'll have arguments just like sisters would," Betty commented. "We understand each other. We're going through the same things together. Every part of our life is almost the same."[6]

Even though Kim had been at Karolyi's since the beginning, she did not feel threatened when new gymnasts like Betty joined the team.

"We all understood that we were all there for the same reason, but it helped us because we were able to see the competition every day in the gym," Kim explained. "It wasn't like you're training by yourself . . . it really helped all of us to push each other, and Betty is my best friend and it hasn't had any effect on our friendship at all. My closest friends are all who I've been in a group with at the gym."[7]

Bela agreed that competition made better athletes. Like Kim, he was also very competitive. "The lowest quality professional performance came of my life when I had no competition,"[8] Bela said. In other words, when the competition stepped up, the results were better.

* * *

After Kim's victorious year in 1990, Bela thought it would be difficult for her to be as successful in 1991 with her present work ethic. Kim had not done well in Europe or in the American Cup.

Bela was not satisfied with her attitude and remarked unhappily, "They have a tendency to relax, to say, 'Well, I'm pretty good, I'm very good, I'm super good, and I'm taking it a little bit easier.' This happened to Kim pretty evidently after the last year of performances." Bela continued, growling, "Unfortunately, her priorities cannot be set right and that messes up, probably, her ultimate goals."[9]

Kim, though, was as determined as ever to capture a major all-around title. She had not won a major title since the United States versus the Soviet Union meet back in August 1990, almost one half year ago.

Three days after the American Cup, Kim traveled to the campus of Georgia Tech University in Atlanta, Georgia, for the 1991 McDonald's International Mixed Pairs meet. In 1990 she had won this competition with her partner, Lance Ringnald. This time, she was paired with Chris Waller. Both had been runners-up at the recent American Cup and had something to prove. This would be their chance to get revenge on Betty and Trent Dimas, since both of them had won the American Cup and were paired together.

Kim chose to show off her new floor routine—which the crowd had been anticipating—in the first rotation. She began with her usual full-twisting double pike somersault and then proceeded to wrap the audience at the Alexander Memorial

Coliseum around her finger as she leaped and danced to *"In the Mood."* Her trademark middle pass of three whip backs to a double tuck somersault was solid. She did a high double tuck somersault to finish, but she had to take a noticeable step back on her landing.

The only thing the routine lacked was a smile. Kim's body movements fit the music, but her face did not. She wore a vacant look throughout the routine. Still, the judges liked it and gave her a 9.925.

The other half of her team, Chris, managed to stay on the nerve-wracking pommel horse for a 9.75. Pommel horse to men is what balance beam is to women.

Betty executed a beautiful uneven bar routine but hopped on her simple barani flyaway dismount for a 9.90. Trent chose his best event to start the competition: the high-flying and thrilling high bar. He dazzled the crowd with his lofty three release moves and a stuck triple back for a 9.80 and the lead.

Kim and Betty both elected to do balance beam in the second round and performed equally well for a 9.90 apiece. The pressure rested on the guys' shoulders, since only one pair from the United States could advance to the next and final rotation. Trent was impressive on the rings and did not falter for a 9.80. Chris waltzed over to high bar and nailed everything, despite the tremendous tension. He ended his routine with a double-twisting double back that worked the audience into a frenzy. He earned slightly more than Trent—a 9.85—to advance his team into the final round.[10]

Kim chose to perform on uneven bars in the third round. Her routine was probably one of the best she had ever performed. She included an excellent Gienger, a high Tkatchev, and a beautiful pike double back dismount in her set for a 9.90. Her partner hit a solid ring routine that enabled them to effortlessly capture the International Mixed Pairs title over

Zhang Xia and Qiao Liang of China. Betty and Trent finished fourth.[11]

Following the Mixed Pairs competition was the International Challenge: United States versus Romania, held April 6 in Kim's hometown of Houston at the Hofheinz Pavilion. Kim was hoping to keep her winning streak alive.

Betty would not be competing due to a pulled hamstring. The day after her injury, Betty had gone through six beam routines and nine bar routines. She had not realized she was injured until the next morning when she woke up and she could not walk. She had gone to practice but had been unable to do anything, leaving Kim as the sole leader for the United States team.

This competition marked a very special time for Bela and his wife Martha because ten years earlier, almost to the day, they had walked out of a New York hotel room on the last day of a tour with Nadia and the Romanian team to defect to the United States. It was ironic that the ten-year anniversary of their defection would occur during the USA versus Romania competition.

Bela remembered very clearly what he was thinking on that day, March 30, 1981: "As soon as we walked out from the hotel, and I looked back, and I said, 'Why am I doing this? Where am I going now?' You might understand forty years of a very sturdy, very secure life. The only thing that socialism gave to the people was the security of tomorrow. You never have to worry . . . no matter if you're even working. So this feeling which was the security was suddenly gone, so I looked around and thought, 'What am I going to do next?'"[12]

Bela, with his wife Martha and his choreographer of seven years, Geza Pozsar, had decided to leave suddenly. Totally unprepared, the Karolyi's had started with only $360 and a big stuffed animal they had purchased for their daughter, Andrea, who was still in Romania. They had found Martha's aunt, who lived in a one room apartment in Manhattan. President Reagan had been shot on Bela's second day of freedom, which left him wondering what kind of mess he had gotten himself into. But ten years later, Bela found himself a wealthy and successful American citizen with a prosperous business and a second home on a spacious ranch.

The USA versus Romania competition was the second head-to-head match with this European country. The first one had been held in 1977 at the New Orleans Superdome. Ironically, Bela had been the Romanian coach, and his team had won. Also, his star pupil, Nadia Comaneci, had captured the all-around. No one would have guessed then that the next time these two teams met in a dual competition, Bela would be the United States coach with a new star pupil: an American, Kim Zmeskal.

Kim did an excellent vault to start off the competition with a 9.933. Chelle Stack and Hilary Grivich also had solid vaults, giving the U.S. team a small lead.

In the second rotation, Kim performed well on uneven bars and had no major errors. She received a 9.916 to put her in first place after two rotations. She was leading Romania's Eugenia Popa and a relatively new face in American gymnastics, Kerri Strug.

Kerri currently trained with Bela in Houston. She had moved in December 1990 from Tucson, Arizona, where she had been coached by Jim Gault, the head women's gymnastics instructor at the University of Arizona.

Kerri was solid on beam until the double back dismount, where inexperience got the best of her and she had to touch her hand to the mat. The judges gave her a 9.466 which was likely to drop her out of the running.

Kim began her beam routine with confidence as she stuck

her tumbling pass and leap series. She hit her back tuck swing down, the same skill that had caused her difficulty in the American Cup. She only took a small hop on the dismount for a 9.933, remaining in the lead with only one event to go.

Shannon Miller helped the United States team with an extremely difficult beam routine that she performed wonderfully for a 9.95. The best Romanian gymnast, Cristina Bontas, fell on a release move on uneven bars, opening the door even wider for Kim and the U.S. team.

On floor exercise, the final event, Hilary Grivich and Shannon Miller had slight errors, but both performed high levels of difficulty, especially for their young ages. Unfortunately, two other Americans fell on floor, so one of their scores—Kim Kelly's 9.25—counted toward the team total. This would hurt the United States' chances of winning.

Kim began her floor routine with a powerful full-twisting double pike somersault. Her routine was so lively that she had the crowd in the palm of her hand as she prepared for her middle pass. This time, she added a fourth whip back before her double back somersault, and the audience went crazy. She went on to stick a high double tuck somersault.

The crowd responded with a standing ovation, and the entire United States team rushed over to congratulate her. Bela and Martha gave her big hugs. The judges gave her a 9.966 which brought loud boos from some of the fans who thought she deserved a 10.

Three judges comprised the panel: one American, one Romanian, and one Canadian (from a neutral country). The Canadian and Romanian judge gave Kim a 9.95 and the American judge gave her a 10. Cristina Bontas received the same floor score as Kim, only the American and Romanian judges' scores were reversed.[13]

Even though the judges did not award a perfect score, Kim

was still able to finish first. Eugenia Popa placed a distant second, and Hilary Grivich and Shannon Miller tied for third.

Tim Daggett, a member of the gold medal-winning 1984 men's Olympic team, interviewed Kim after the meet. He asked Kim about the hometown crowd, and she smiled.

"It was really nice having it in front of a home crowd and knowing basically almost all the audience. That helps a lot," she said.

Tim then asked if she thought she would score a 10 on floor. She replied, "Yeah, it felt pretty good, but it's not my decision, and I did my best."

When asked if it was difficult to compete on the final event knowing the team would not win, Kim responded, "Yeah, but it doesn't matter; we showed that we're pulling up."

Bela said of Kim's victory, "My heart is just up and growing from the happiness." But the team competition was another story. He frowned and said, "The same [time] I'm sharing the sadness of the defeat along with them. And I don't like it. I hate it. I'm a bad loser. But with all these things together, I have to tell I'm part of the performance and I feel it and I don't want to hide it."[14]

Kim and the United States team had an opportunity at the meet to get to know the Romanian team a little better. With the crumbling of communism, the Romanians were much more friendly and open during competitions.

"Fortunately, Betty does speak and understand Romanian," Kim said. "It has made communicating with the Romanian team much easier. Thanks to Betty, we've gotten the opportunity to learn more about these athletes, as well as their lives in a country very different from our own."[15]

* * *

The next meet on Kim's agenda was the 1991 U.S. Championships held June 6-9 at the Shoemaker Center in Cincinnati, Ohio. Kim returned to the Championships as the defending all-around winner and was favored to win the competition despite a nagging wrist injury. Betty Okino was not competing due to a stress fracture in her elbow brought about by overcompensating for her pulled hamstring.

During the compulsories, Mike Jacki, the executive director of the United States Gymnastics Federation, gave Bela a warning for protesting Kim's vault score. Kim had taken a small hop after her Yamashita half and the judges had given her a 9.85. Bela was furious. Mike threatened to kick Bela out of the competition if he did it again. He also told Bela to just worry about coaching, and he would take care of the rest.

"He is a supreme student of the game," Mike said about Bela. "He runs around yelling at the judges and complaining about the scoring, but he never takes his eyes off his girls. In the meantime, the other coaches are all watching Bela and ignoring their own kids."[16]

Randi Hall interviewed Bela regarding Kim's condition prior to the optionals. Randi asked if Kim would be in pain.

Bela, a little unhappy with Kim's preparation for this meet, responded flatly, "She will be in pain no question about it. She was in pain yesterday, she will be in even bigger [pain] today. Optionals is much harder than the compulsories, but she is a tough girl with a strong character, and I am expecting her to pull through this competition just like many, many other ones in the past. I hope she's going to win it."[17]

Bela's unsympathetic attitude revealed that there were some problems brewing between him and his star pupil. Kim was very opinionated and she was not afraid to let Bela know. If his views differed from hers, they often clashed.

Kim described their relationship this way: "Me and Bela

71

are both—I don't know what's the word—strong-willed, I guess. I always think I'm right, and he always thinks he's right. Sometimes we kind of butt heads. But, you know, I guess that's gotten me where I'm at, too." She laughed and added, "He usually wins, though."[18]

Kim realized the importance of good communication. "Communication between coaches and athletes is crucial," Kim explained. "My relationship with Bela has always been a positive one. If he gets mad at me because I'm making mistakes, I remind myself that he is just trying to better my performance."[19]

Bela thought Kim's training for recent meets had not been adequate, and he was not satisfied with her fluctuating weight. At these National Championships she weighed eighty-two pounds and was four feet six-and-a-half inches tall. This may not seem like a lot, but gymnasts need to be small and light in order to lift their body weight and flip. The extra weight means extra pounding on one's joints, which can lead to more injuries.

Bela believed Kim's wrist injury was more the result of a mental condition than a physical one. "Yes, I am definitely disappointed, more disappointed with [Kim] than with Betty because Betty's is an unfortunate injury, an athletic injury," he explained. "Her [Kim's] injury is mostly coming out from attitude rather than physical."

"I don't just want to go by and make the World Championship team, or whatever, and just be there," Kim emphasized in an interview. "I want to be the best. I wouldn't be spending so much time in the gym if I didn't want to be in the World Championships and the Olympics."

"She wants to be in it, she wants to be successful, no question about it. I have no doubt in my mind," Bela agreed. "The only problem, she can't keep up the priorities strong enough in front of her to . . . work with all the small details to work in reaching the goal. And those details are very important."

Kim had admitted on many occasions in the past that she preferred competition to workouts. She did much better under pressure than in everyday practice sessions. Bela would sometimes get mad in practice if Kim was not doing well enough, and he would kick her out of the gym. Fiery Kim would just stand there boldly and tell Bela she wanted to stay. Sometimes Bela would give in and give her a second chance, and other times he would not.

Despite the simmering quarrel between Bela and Kim, she began the U.S. Championships as the forerunner after compulsories with a slight lead over Kim Kelly of the Parkettes in Allentown, Pennsylvania.

Kim began on beam. She worked smoothly and with confidence. Her tumbling passes were very steady, but she took a small hop on the dismount.

Kim walked toward Bela, and he cupped her head in his hands, commenting, "That's how it is supposed to look like, a good routine. Good job."

Martha chimed in as she patted Kim on the head, "Good job, Kimbo." The judges gave Kim a 9.80.

Her next event was the floor exercise. She had not practiced her routine much because of her aching wrist, but that did not stop her from opening with a high full-twisting double pike. She stepped out of bounds on her middle pass but finished strong for another 9.80.

Kim turned in a good vault to keep herself ahead of the field. She was performing admirably, especially since she had strained ligaments in her left wrist.

The final event—uneven bars—would be Kim's toughest. She had been having trouble just grabbing the bar because of her aching wrist, so she had not performed a full routine during practice the week before the meet.

Kim spoke about the pain she was enduring and how she was dealing with it: "It's been hurting me quite a bit, but I just try to block out the pain. I just keep thinking one more routine and then I'll be finished."

Kim chalked her hands to prepare for her bar routine while Bela gave her some last minute instructions. She refused to look at him while he talked. The problems between the two continued even though she was ahead of the competition. Throughout the meet, Bela spent much more time coaching Kerri Strug than he did coaching Kim, as if he was punishing her by ignoring her.

Kim used a conservative bar routine with only one release move. She had a slight error on a full-twisting giant, but her routine was still good enough to make her the two-time National Champion. The last American to repeat as National Champion had been Tracee Talavera in 1982.

Bela gave Kim a hug and congratulated her, shaking her hand and saying, "Grand champion. Good job, Kimbo."

Kerri Strug did an excellent routine to place third behind Sandy Woolsey. While her routine was well done, she omitted a difficult full-twisting double flyaway dismount and substituted an easier one for it. This move may have cost her the championship.

Randi Hall interviewed Kim after the meet. She asked Kim if winning even while injured made it more satisfying.

"Yeah," Kim replied, "it does, because I had to change my bar routine at the last minute, and I only did like one or two full floor routines before this, and it means a lot that I could pull it out when I had to."

Kim shared what changes she intended to make for the World Championships: "I'm planning on making some more difficult tumbling passes, and my bar routine will go back to what it was before I just changed it real quick."[20]

In the event finals the next day, Kim elected to compete in only two events, balance beam and floor exercise. She qualified to all four apparatus finals but decided not to do vault and uneven bars because of her sprained wrist.

Randi Hall asked Bela for his thoughts regarding Kim's competition status. He remarked, "I had a very serious thought about pulling her out of this competition. Despite her injury, she did perform very well yesterday. [She] pulled to the end and won the champion title, but today is the event finals. I was thinking very seriously and finally I thought, 'Give her the chance to go for two events.' I pulled her out from vault and bars, the two very difficult events for her arm."

Kim mounted the beam wearing the same colorful blue and white leotard she had worn at the 1990 U.S. Championships in Denver. Her routine was excellent and free from any major errors. The judges gave her a 9.812, which placed her second behind Shannon Miller.

Kim wowed the crowd with a nearly perfect performance on floor exercise. She tied for first place with Dominique Dawes of Hill's Angels in Gaithersburg, Maryland. Each scored a 9.912.

Kim was asked about the pressure of following a good performance like Dominique Dawes's floor routine. She replied, "I think it's better to go after a better routine, because then you know what you have to beat, instead of when you go first, the people behind you get the chance to see what's coming."[21]

After the meet, Kim and her teammates went home. For the remainder of the summer, Bela took all his best gymnasts—Kim, Betty Okino, Kerri Strug, and Hilary Grivich—to his ranch. Located in Waverly Hills about fifty miles north of

Houston in the beautiful Sam Houston National Forest, it was a good place to train for the World Championships.

At the ranch there was a relatively new 25,000 square foot gymnasium capable of training gymnasts at all skill levels, from beginners to Olympians. To relax, the athletes could swim in the Olympic-sized pool, play tennis, or ride horses.

Bela enjoyed riding his horse around the ranch in jeans, a flannel shirt, and cowboy boots. He had stumbled upon the land in 1983 after becoming lost rabbit hunting. After saving his money for a year, he had coaxed the owner to sell.

Bela liked being a cowboy. "My all time hero is John Wayne,"[22] he admitted.

While the ranch was fun, Kim found it difficult to be away from her family. "I don't know how the other girls do it, staying away from their parents," Kim said, "because my parents have helped me out a whole lot in my gymnastics, just being there for me."

Betty, on the other hand, lived in Houston with her sixty-nine-year-old grandmother, Anna Mattei, who had moved to Houston to live with her granddaughter while she trained at Karolyi's. Anna cooked the meals at the ranch to help pay for Betty's stay.

"She means a lot to me," Betty observed about her grandmother, "because if it wasn't for her, I don't know if I would have made it through this past year. Because I've had a lot of injuries, and she helped me get through those, too, and also the workouts and everything has gotten harder since the 1992 Olympics are closer and closer and the World Championships are just around the corner. So it's gotten tougher, and I needed somebody here with me."[23]

Betty's parents lived in a suburb of Chicago, and she did not get to see them very often. They talked on the phone quite frequently, though, sometimes as much as three times a day.

The practice sessions at the ranch were intense and demanding. Bela insisted, "You have to have total dedication, you have to spend hours, you have to be focused, you have to make some sacrifices. Gosh, nothing in the world can [be obtained] without sacrifices, especially when you want to get something which is the best in the world. You have to pull the most out of you, the most, more than anybody else. That's the name of the game."[24]

Kim took Bela's advice to heart, saying, "As long as I just do my best and keep training hard, I know things will turn out there [at the World Championships]."[25]

The humidity during the summer in Houston was almost unbearable at times. The long training sessions in the heat made the kids tired, thirsty, and hungry.

"I wonder what's for lunch. I hope it's good," Kim would mumble after a hard workout as the girls headed toward the cafeteria.

While staying at the ranch, the girls relied on each other for support since their families were absent.

"I think all of us have grown up a bit faster than most kids our age because of what we have to go through, but inside we're still little kids, I guess," Kim said. "Luckily, all of us get along really well. We're all going through the same thing, so we help each other."[26]

The training at the ranch ended just prior to the World Championships. Kim spent a little time with her family the evening before she left for the competition. She packed her leotards, gymnastics hair ribbons, and makeup in a suitcase as her younger sister, Melissa, sat sadly next to her on the bed.

Kim's bedroom was light-colored and reflected her young age. Above her bed on the headboard, many stuffed animals were displayed. A New Kids on the Block poster was hanging beside her bed.

Kim said she liked Bart Simpson "a little, [but] not too much anymore." She perked up, "I'm a New Kids on the Block fan, though." They were her favorite music group, and she hoped to see them perform live. "She [Mary Lou] just went to a concert and she got to meet them," Kim said enthusiastically. "So the next time they come, she's going to try to get everyone in, but we don't know yet."[27]

Kim was almost finished packing when her mom called, "Hey girls, how are you all doing? Getting everything packed up?"

"Yeah," the girls quietly mumbled. Kim's younger sister missed spending time with her and did not want to see her go.

Kim's mother longed to spend time with her as well. "She's a very tender-hearted person, and she loves being at home," Clarice Zmeskal said of her oldest child. "And I think she wishes that she could be there with us more often, too. And I really miss having that. You know, she's a fifteen-year-old, and we've never really shared any teenage years together, yet."[28]

Kim admitted that with her busy workout and travel schedule, "Sometimes family get-togethers happen without me."[29] But she had to put all those feelings aside for now and focus completely on the World Championships.

Bela looked forward to the challenge of the competition. "No question, absolutely, this is the best, the strongest, and most aggressive group I've had,"[30] he boasted.

Bela's girls were usually undaunted in competition and were capable of giving the Soviets and Romanians a run for their money. The home advantage might be just enough to push the Americans over the edge and into the limelight, making gymnastics history in the process.

A young Kim contemplating her meet strategy.

Kim performing for the crowd at the 1990 U.S. Challenge.

Kim shows a nice scale during her compulsory beam routine.

Bela helps Kim before her first U.S. Championships by pinning the number on her back.

Kim works confidently on the balance beam in Las Vegas.

Graceful Kim flows through her compulsory floor exercise routine.

Kim briefly holds a pose before flipping down the beam.

Kim soars above the top bar on her Tkatchev release move.

Kim looks to catch the bar on her Tkatchev.

After capturing her second national title, Kim plays to the audience during the event finals in Cincinnati.

Kim listens intently to Bela's advice.

Kim displays a pretty flyaway full dismount off the uneven bars in Denver.

Kim mounts the balance beam while trying to block out the pain in her sprained left wrist during the 1991 U.S. Championships.

Kim executes a full split on her leap.

Kim's trademark ending pose on floor.

Bela gives Kim a big bear hug for a job well done.

Kim breezes through the compulsory floor routine in the team competition of the 1991 World Championships in Indianapolis.

The silver medal-winning U.S. team at the 1991 World Championships (left to right: Betty Okino, Michelle Campi, Hilary Grivich,
Kerri Strug, Shannon Miller, and Kim).

Kim shows off her *"In the Mood"* floor routine during the all-around competition in Indianapolis.

Bela is ecstatic that Kim has won the 1991 World Championships.

Kim on top of the world. Svetlana Boginskaya is second and
Cristina Bontas is third.

Kim Zmeskal, the *first* American ever to win the all-around in a World Championships.

Chapter 5

CONQUERING THE WORLD

In mid-August, when other teenagers were preparing to return to school after their summer break, Kim left for Indianapolis to attend one of the biggest meets of her career: the 1991 World Championships (sometimes called "Worlds"). As this year's Worlds were to be held in the year immediately prior to the Olympic Games, the competitive field would be tough, experienced, and in top shape. Winning these Worlds so close to the Olympics would make a gymnast well known in the judges' eyes and a heavy favorite in Barcelona.

The United States team was selected August 24, 1991, just a few weeks prior to the World Championships. Kim was a shoo-in for the team. She performed very well before a small private audience and made the first cut along with Betty Okino, Kerri Strug, Shannon Miller, Hilary Grivich, Sandy Woolsey, and the two alternates: Elisabeth Crandall and Michelle Campi. The top four placements from the meet made the team; the other two spots were up for grabs and would be decided over the next several weeks during the training sessions where two of the eight would be cut.

The squad practiced at the USGF training center to tune up and get in some last minute preparation before the World Championships. Elisabeth Crandall, the seventh spot, was removed from the team because she had a sore calf, narrowing the team down to seven gymnasts.

Just prior to the meet, there were two podium workouts: one for compulsories and one for optionals. The podium practices helped the gymnasts get acquainted with the surroundings and get used to competing on elevated equipment. For many of the young U.S. gymnasts, this was their first time competing on a podium, the same setup that would be used for the Olympics.

Shortly before the competition began, the coaches of the seven gymnasts met and voted on either Michelle or Sandy for the sixth position. All the coaches, except Sandy's, voted for Michelle. Michelle had actually placed eighth during the private competition in August, but the coaches liked her style and thought the judges would appreciate it too, so they decided to bump Sandy out of the sixth spot and use Michelle instead.

The controversial selection process hurt Sandy and angered her coach, Stormy Eaton. Sandy had been on the 1989 World Championship team and had participated in major international competitions, such as the 1990 Goodwill Games. By contrast, Michelle had no international experience, but she had been coached by Bela at one time and now was coached by Geza Pozsar. Interestingly, the only gymnast who made the final team but had never been coached by Bela was Shannon Miller.

Despite the controversy surrounding the team selection process, Bela looked forward to the challenge of the World Championships. "Oh boy," he grunted, "it's gonna be a dogfight, a dogfight I tell you! We have a great team, a great group of kids with fighting spirit and strong will. This is a very fine group of athletes that will represent our country in Indianapolis . . . I guarantee the U.S. girls will be in the hunt for medals and will take event medals."[1]

Before the team competition, Bela spoke of his hopes for the United States team: "A bronze or silver in this very competition would really comfort everybody, would really give a great pride, being a . . . medal winner in a World Championship. By the time, as individual athletes, being just an individual, an isolated individual, they would never be around anything like that before. So in this way, they have a very good incentive to work toward a perfect goal, and that is the team competition medal, which . . . puts in second place any kind of personal egos or ambitions. Sure, we are not lining them up like chess figurines on the table. We are talking to them, we are saying 'That's the way we think, we feel,' like, you know, we are going to be a vision. 'That's the way we are going to force the medal out, that's the way you are going to make yourself very proud.' They are young enough and they are innocent enough to feel comfortable in each other's shadow, in each other's vicinity, in each other's help, and also they feel much more powerful and as a unit than isolated individuals."

Bela was a great motivator and able to make adolescents determined and focused. He said, "It is so interesting with this young generation, [at] this very typical age of fourteen or fifteen. You would think, 'Ah well, they're going to be shaky, they're going to be concerned.' No, that is the type of age when they are not concerned with anything else. They are not concerned because they do not have anything to hold on to. They do not have great backgrounds or great achievements already, so they are relaxed, they are hungry, they have nothing to lose. They go for it."[2]

KIM ZMESKAL

The 1991 World Championships were held September 6-15 in Indianapolis. These Worlds, which at the time were every two years, had not been held in the United States since 1979 in Fort Worth, Texas. Having this competition on their home soil would be advantageous to the Americans. The environment, not to mention the fans, would be in their favor.

Kim liked the pressure-filled situation of being in the spotlight and having the crowd cheering. "I think it helps me when I know I have to do it," she said. "I don't get so relaxed and have it slip away from me. I think it helps, especially when you're in the United States, to have the crowd behind you. It's a nice feeling."[3]

The format of the World Championships was the same as that of the Olympics. The first part was the team compulsories and the second part was the team optionals. Whichever team had the highest total after both competitions won. The third part was the all-around final to decide the best gymnast. The fourth and final part was the individual event finals. Gymnasts only competed on the events to which they qualified.

In the team compulsories, Hilary Grivich and Kerri Strug got the American team off to a good start with strong performances in the first round. (Only two gymnasts per country competed in each round.) Kim and Betty Okino would compete in the next session on Sunday evening, September 8. Bela had placed Kim and Betty in this particular session because he believed the large crowd would enhance their performance and possibly their score. The crowd was expected to be a lot smaller in the final session on Monday morning when Michelle Campi and Shannon Miller would be competing.

Kim began on vault. She panicked briefly, thinking, "Oh my gosh, this is the World Championships." She later admitted, "This was the most nervous I've gotten in a while, but then I thought of it as any other meet."

82

Overcoming her jitters, Kim executed a strong vault, but she could not stick the landing. This earned her a 9.775. Next, she moved to uneven bars. Her bar routine was clean, and she ended with an impressive flyaway full dismount. The judges gave her a 9.787. She completed her beam routine without any major errors for a 9.875 and danced expressively on floor for a 9.837.

After the compulsory round of the team competition, the United States was a surprising second behind the Soviet Union.

Bela was thrilled. "We are not focusing on winning the competition," he said. "Right now we are in second place and we are happy with this. We can give a very strong competition to anybody in the first four places."[4]

The team with the highest score after compulsories began on vault, the team with the second highest score began on bars, the third place team began on beam, and the fourth place team began on floor. Thus, the higher up a team placed, the better their order of competition in the optionals.

The United States started on the uneven bars with a solid effort. Kim was last up. She performed both her release moves, Gienger and Tkatchev, excellently and stuck her dismount—like most of her teammates had done so far—for a 9.912. All of the Americans hit their bar routines to maintain their slim lead over Romania. The Soviet Union performed outstanding amounts of difficulty almost flawlessly to give them a large lead early in the competition.

The U.S. team moved to balance beam. The order was almost the same as in the previous event, with Kim last. Again, all the Americans stayed on the apparatus and executed wonderful routines. Kim had no major mistakes, and she stuck the dismount for a 9.95.

The United States went to floor with a lead of about two tenths of a point over the Romanians. There were some minor problems: Michelle Campi stepped out of bounds on her first tumbling run, and Hilary Grivich had a fall on her opening tumbling pass. But the lowest score on each event could be dropped, so the United States still had a chance to beat the Romanians as long as everyone else hit. With the pressure on, Betty Okino, Kerri Strug, and Shannon Miller all successfully executed their routines. Only Kim was left.

Bart Conner interviewed Kim's parents just prior to her floor exercise routine. "We're just very proud of them, just very excited, and I'm a nervous wreck,"[5] laughed Kim's mom, Clarice.

Kim performed one of her best routines, nailing all her tumbling passes without a hitch. The crowd at the Hoosier Dome was elated, showing support with a standing ovation. The cheers turned to boos, however, when a score of 9.95 was flashed on the scoreboard; they wanted a 10.

The final rotation began with the Americans in a tie with Romania. The Soviets were solidly in first place. The battle would be for the silver.

"I was a little scared knowing we were tied," Kim said, "because we had been ahead of the Romanians for the whole competition."

The Americans all executed the same vault and most of them stuck the landing. On the other side of the arena, the Romanians were completing all of their bars sets with excellent polish and class. The excitement was building. The crowd was being treated to the world's elite in gymnastics who were performing to the best of their abilities.

Kim was last up, and the audience was anxiously anticipating her performance. "I was very excited, especially because I knew I could help the team,"[6] Kim remembered thinking before her final event.

She did a great first vault for a 9.962. At the exact

moment she landed, the final competitor for Romania, Lavinia Milosovici, fell from the uneven bars. It looked good for the United States and the silver medal.

Kim glanced at Bela. They seemed to be on the same wavelength; she understood his language and hand gestures.

"Go strong," he reminded her, "do what we've been practicing, and mostly stay down on the landing."[7]

Kim knew how important it was to land properly. Bela had told her many times that the last major impression left on the judges' minds came from the landing.

Kim peered down the runway before her second vault and saluted the judges while deep in concentration. She glanced at her starting marker one more time, then she sprinted down the mat. She exploded off the springboard, soared through the air—reminiscent of Mary Lou in 1984—and landed without moving an inch. Bela threw his hands up in the air and rushed to hug the entire team. Then they all turned and waited for the score: a 10 was flashed, and the spectators went crazy, applauding on their feet and waving banners for the U.S. team. What an achievement for American gymnastics!

Bela picked up the four-foot six-inch Kim and tossed her into the air. Her body looked like a flying rag doll in contrast to Bela, a six-foot one-inch giant.

The scoreboard told the story; it showed Kim's perfect score next to Lavinia Milosovici's 9.412. In a thrilling battle, the United States had clinched the silver medal for the first time ever in World Championship history. The Soviets, like many times in the past, won the gold, and Romania had to settle for the bronze.

"This silver medal feels great," Kim sighed. "I don't even know what to say, I feel so relieved."[8]

Bart Conner interviewed Kim after the competition. "This is so amazing," she beamed, "we're just so happy that we won the silver. That means so much to us." Bart asked Kim if the home crowd helped and Kim answered, "Oh yeah, the crowd helped a lot, especially since I was last up on all the events. Sometimes it's hard to keep yourself motivated, but with this crowd behind us it was really easy." When asked if it felt good to accomplish this heading into 1992, Kim replied, "This feels wonderful. I just hope we can repeat it and even do better next year."

Bart found Bela and asked him what kind of message he was sending. Bela exclaimed, "The message is out there, the closed chain of the Socialist domination in women's gymnastics is broken forever! We got the place and we're going to hold on to it as long as humanly can be done. And I believe we're sending a great message to our program, the American program, our kids tomorrow. I know millions of young ones are going to want [to do] gymnastics and are going to want to turn into another Kim Zmeskal, Betty Okino, Shannon Miller, and all those ones who have been fighting so hard today."

Bart said many people had thought Bela could not build a winning team in this country. "Well, that was the mentality when we came here, you remember," Bela replied, "because we have been forces from the beginning. But I'm proud. Yes, wherever in the world, no matter where you go, if you are taking the kids right, if you're holding them right, showing the light—'that is the light, we can reach it, we can make it'—they'll follow you. There is no mistake, they don't want to be participants. Everybody will want to work to be a winner. And as long as they are leaning upright, they're going to be the winners. It's a great day. It's a great day!"[9]

Although they had easily won the gold, the Soviets were outraged. Their head coach, Alexander Alexandrov, fumed, "The judges were very generous to the Americans, especially in the vault. Lisenko did a double-twisting Yurchenko and received a 9.975. Zmeskal did a single-twisting Yurchenko and got a 10. I feel this was unfair."[10] Normally, the Soviets were the ones accused of getting extra tenths from the judges, especially when the competition was in their homeland.

The Romanians were also upset. Their head coach, Octavian Belu, refused to go to the press conference after the meet. Despite their outrage, the Romanians were fortunate to get the bronze since they had been plagued by many errors in the compulsory segment of the team competition.

Although much controversy surrounded the scoring, many steps had been taken to provide the fairest judging possible. Each of the major powers in gymnastics had been represented by judges from that country. The judges had been tracked on computer to see if anyone was consistently high or low. Any judge found guilty of being biased would have been ejected from the competition. Six judges had been used, with the highest and lowest scores dropped and the middle four averaged.

Even with these efforts to make this subjective sport more objective, the scoring had been subject to the same problems that affect the judging of any major competition. Gymnasts who had won in the past and had made a name for themselves usually benefitted from their reputation with favorable scores, even for average performances. Placement in the lineup during the team competition was also key to receiving a high score. Typically, the first girl up from a certain country was a consistent but less known gymnast who in a sense was sacrificed for the good of the team. The last spot was usually reserved for the best gymnast, with the others falling in between according to ability. The judges knew this, so they left room for higher scores. If the judges awarded a 10 to the first girl up, but someone else on the team performed even better, there would be no way to give a higher score.

When asked about the monitoring of the judges during the World Championships, Bela said, "I'm not 100 percent sure this did work. I'm not 100 percent [sure] it will ever work. Judges are doing the same thing just like before . . . but nobody had a word about the notorious cheaters, the Soviets. The Romanian judge was outrageously favorizing her own team, killing everybody on [scores]. They did not mention anything about the Chinese coalition who was with the Japanese talking throughout the competition, setting the score right where they wanted it to be set." Bela continued, "I don't believe the whole system is really having any kind of efficiency, but I just thought any tendency, any try, any struggle in order to set up better a more [objective] appreciation among the judges on behalf of the gymnasts is welcome to see, and I personally applaud."[11]

The Soviets were not totally poor sports. "I want to congratulate the American team," Alexander Alexandrov said. "They have a very good and fine and interesting team."

Bela was pleased with his team's performance, but he still saw room for improvement. "I hope in the future we'll give [the Soviets] a harder run for their money and especially for the gold money," he commented. "From now on the world [has] got to count on us."[12]

Julie Moran asked Nadia for her opinion of the current United States team. "Well, they changed a lot [since] the last time," she said, referring to the improvements the United States had made since their fourth place finish in the 1989 World Championships. "Gymnastics is not the same as in '76," Nadia continued. "The things I did in '76 were very hard at that time, but they warm-up with this now."

Julie also asked Nadia why Bela was so successful. "Well, because he is the best coach in the world," Nadia replied. "I said this, and I will all the time say this."[13]

Conquering the World

* * *

The all-around final followed the team competition and was held on Friday, the 13th of September. Kim was hoping that this would be her lucky day, despite the superstitions surrounding the calendar date. Next to the Olympics, this would be the fiercest competition Kim would ever face.

Kim's parents made the trip to Indianapolis. They attended most of Kim's meets. On the day of the all-around final, they did not get a chance to see Kim before the competition because, as usual, Bela was with the kids preparing them mentally.

"The day of the meet is very nerve-racking to me," Clarice Zmeskal said. "I pace the floor a lot. My stomach is up to my throat; I get very nervous for her."

"You feel very nervous for her," admitted Kim's dad, David. "You know she is prepared. You'd like to be out there helping her, but you know you can't. You have to sit back as a parent and watch her from the stands." In a voice filled with emotion, he added, "She'll always be my little girl."

David and Clarice browsed in local stores to keep their minds off the upcoming competition. "We do a lot of shopping," Clarice said. "We go around looking at different things and try to keep away from the subject of gymnastics—as much as possible," she added as they stumbled across a picture of Kim in a store window promoting the World Championships. Kim's mom liked the picture of Kim on the balance beam.

"I like the gold [medals] right above her," David said quietly.

Kim's mother agreed. "I hope we end up with the gold tonight."

Kim's dad nodded and said, "You bet."[14]

While the Zmeskal's were out shopping, Bela watched his athletes closely. He monitored what they ate during competitions. Kim had to pay attention to her diet to keep in top form. For breakfast before a meet, she would eat something light, like yogurt and a banana. For lunch, she would eat some kind of chicken or fish. Dinners during the week of the big competition would often consist of spaghetti for energy, although she would not eat dinner on the day of the competition until after the meet. When it was all over, Kim would have a light meal like chicken, vegetables, and a salad. It was usually quite late in the evening, and Bela did not want to stuff his athletes full of food. There would be little activity after the meal, and no calories would be burned off.

To qualify to the all-around final, a gymnast must place in the top thirty-six during the team competition, and only three gymnasts per country may advance. The top three for the United States were Kim, Betty Okino, and Shannon Miller.

"My goal was just to do the best job I could, and I was really shooting for any medal," Kim said. "I really wanted to get at least a bronze in the all-around."[15]

Bela pinned Kim's assigned number, 151, on the back of her leotard. The leotard was white with a blue star on the front next to her right shoulder. The number would be used by the judges and volunteers at the score table who tallied the results.

Kim began on the vault. Her first vault was very good for a 9.925. The second vault was an exact replica of the one she had performed perfectly in the team competition. This time she received a 9.962 and took the early lead. One reason for the lower score was that vault was her first event, and the judges needed to leave room to give higher scores to those gymnasts performing a double-twisting Yurchenko. Both double-twisting and single-twisting Yurchenkos were valued at a 10, meaning that if the gymnast performed perfectly, she would earn a 10. Some less difficult vaults were valued at a lower score like a 9.80, so if the gymnast performed one perfectly, the highest score she could receive was a 9.80.

This rule applies to all the events. A gymnast must have a certain level of difficulty to have a routine with a starting value of 10. The problem with the system is that the younger gymnasts are constantly raising the amount of difficulty and inventing new skills for their routines. For example, a full-twisting Yurchenko vault used to be valued at a 10; gymnasts then started doing double-twisting Yurchenkos. How could the judges reward a gymnast for doing the more difficult skill? They began valuing the double-twisting Yurchenko at a 10, and lowered the value of the full-twisting Yurchenko. This was done after the 1992 Olympics, when the Code of Points, which determines the value of each skill, was rewritten. Every four years the Code was updated to include new skills and change the value of old ones.

The eighteen-year-old defending World Champion, Svetlana Boginskaya, began on the balance beam. Svetlana was the leader after the team competition, but scores did not carry over, and each gymnast started with a clean slate in the all-around final. Svetlana hit all her skills: back handspring to two layouts, gainer layout, and double back dismount, with only a slight wobble on the landing. She was a little cautious overall but still earned a 9.912.

Svetlana moved to the floor exercise. Known as the "Belorussian Swan," her unique dance and interpretation of the music had won many medals and sparked much attention. She began her floor routine with a high pike full-twisting double back. The crowd was intrigued by her dance. She completed her one-and-a-half twist through to double back and double pike dismount without any problems for a 9.95.

Kim's next event was the uneven bars. This would be her biggest challenge, as she had been having difficulty staying on the apparatus in the past and needed a strong performance to capture the all-around title.

"Kim's last up on bars; she's about having a heart attack about that,"[16] Kim's mom remarked about her position in the order of competitors. Although being last would be advantageous in terms of scoring, she would have to wait a long time. It would be tough to keep loose and warm, as it would be awhile since she had last touched the equipment.

When the time came, Kim executed a high Gienger, then a nice Tkatchev, and landed well her pike double flyaway. That earned her a 9.937 and a big hug from Bela.

Kim recalled her feelings after her bar routine: "They were putting the standings up after every event. I specifically remember after bars—it was my second event and bars is usually my toughest event to compete—and being in first after bars was like, 'Wow, you really have a chance at this one.'"[17]

Meanwhile, Svetlana, wearing the same white leotard with red and yellow stripes that she had worn at the 1989 World Championships, hit a near-perfect vault for a 9.95. On her second attempt she bettered it slightly for a 9.962.

Kim had a very slim lead over Svetlana. She needed to hit one of the best balance beam routines of her life to remain in the lead of this talented group of individuals.

Bela placed the springboard in the proper position, and Kim checked it one last time to make sure it was correct. She raised her arms to salute the judges and bounced off the board with her legs flying up into a v-shape before she lowered them beside the beam. Kim pressed up to a reverse planche and held it for a few seconds. Her back was bent so far that her foot almost touched her head. Her front handspring to a split jump was solid. She prepared for her tumbling pass with a brief pause to concentrate, then she flipped down the sixteen-and-a-half-foot beam and landed without a wobble. She executed two difficult switch leaps in a row, but her arms faltered a little on her gainer layout. However, she made up for it by sticking her double back dismount.

The crowd cheered. Martha and Bela both hugged Kim, but she was still in a very solemn mood. The judges gave her a 9.962 and she kept her lead with one event to go: the floor exercise.

In second place, Svetlana lifted one arm to show she was ready to begin on uneven bars, possibly her weakest event. She did a good full pirouette into a Tkatchev and finished with a double pike flyaway. The routine had no form errors, although she took out one of her major release moves, which lowered her amount of difficulty. The judges gave her a 9.912, and Svetlana scowled. Several audience members whistled and booed; they did not like the score, either.

Bela and Kim went over some last-minute strategy as she got ready for her best event, the floor exercise. He told her to be normal like in practice and not do anything different. "Do what you do every day," he said, "maybe even a little better."[18]

Svetlana decided to leave the arena and not watch Kim's performance. Kim walked up the stairs and stepped onto the podium to prepare for her final routine.

"I was really excited," she explained later to Julie Moran. "I was nervous for the light to go on—it couldn't happen fast enough—and I had a feeling I was going to do a good routine anyway."[19] As she waited for the judges to post the previous gymnast's score, the hyped crowd performed a wave, which pumped up her already high energy level.

Kim exploded off the floor like a rocket on her opening tumbling run. She landed perfectly and smiled at the spectators. She played to the crowd and people clapped and cheered loudly to encourage her. Bela grunted anxiously as Kim went through her second tumbling pass.

Kim's mother, Clarice, worried out loud, "Come on baby,

stick this one. Don't step out of bounds."[20]

Kim knocked off her three whip backs to a double back with ease, and the crowd went wild. All she had left was her final tumbling pass, a double tuck.

Kim said to herself as she prepared for her closing sequence, "I just have one last tumbling pass and this whole thing's over, and it could be me that gets to stand on the podium."[21] She ran hard, soared through the air, and finished with another perfect landing. She threw her arms and head back to accentuate the landing.

The deafening roar from the crowd of 15,000 echoed throughout the Hoosier Dome. The fans rose to their feet as Kim finished her routine. She ran to Bela.

"Yahaa! You've done it!" he yelled while giving her a huge hug and lifting her up so she could wave to her admiring fans, who continued to stand and applaud in recognition of her efforts.

Kim's parents were overjoyed. Her mom exclaimed, "All right! Yes!" and she hugged her husband.

Bela told Kim to wave to the public, and she did. After what seemed like an eternity, the judges flashed a 9.987, and Kim became the first ever American World Champion.

Kim remembered thinking, "I was almost scared to look up at the score, because I wasn't sure if I heard it right."[22] Slowly, she realized that she had won. "It took a long time for it to sink in, and I remember when Hilary Grivich came up to me after the competition and she was like, 'Kim, you won! You won!' I was about to cry. It didn't really seem possible."

Svetlana Boginskaya lost by a little over one tenth to Kim. Cristina Bontas of Romania placed third. Betty Okino stuck her second vault for a 9.937, but that was not enough for her to advance in the standings, and she finished fourth. Shannon Miller, the other American competing, was sixth.

Kim was in a daze. "Even afterward it didn't seem real," she said. "I was almost scared to go up on the podium when they called my name, because I thought that it was like I was dreaming this, that I really didn't belong there."[23]

"I could see in the back of my head the 1984 Olympics," Kim recalled. "I could see Mary Lou standing up there for a second. And then I thought, 'Oh my goodness, this is me up here.'"[24]

What a proud moment for American gymnastics when the red, white, and blue flag was raised and the national anthem was played. Kim smiled and quietly sang the words, while Bela glanced up at the awards stand and nodded his head with a warm smile of approval.

Bela was celebrating his forty-ninth birthday on the day of the all-around final, and Kim had given him the best birthday present of all.

"I never been happier in [my] whole life," Bela exclaimed, "in [my] whole coaching career. It is the greatest moment because this moment put U.S. gymnastics in a whole new arena."[25]

Kathy Johnson interviewed the new World Champion after the meet. She asked Kim if, in her wildest dreams, she thought she could win gold. Kim responded, "Yeah, in my dreams, but realistically I was thinking of going for a silver or bronze. I just can't believe it. I don't know if I want to cry or laugh or I don't know." Kathy stressed how important it was to stick the landing. Kim agreed, "Yeah, that's really important. I've watched a lot of the competitions on television, and that's usually what it came down to."[26]

Once again, the Soviet and Romanian coaches complained about the scoring. The all-around bronze medalist, Cristina Bontas of Romania, did not show up at the press conference following the meet.

"I am 100 percent sure I would have won if the Championships were held in Europe," Svetlana Boginskaya whined arrogantly.

Bela did not agree with that statement. "Svetlana Boginskaya is a beautiful World Champion," he said, "but her time is over."

Unfortunately, Kim was the one most hurt by the others' gripes. Kim found herself defending the title she had worked so hard to attain. She was not the one responsible for the scores, and people were looking to her for some kind of explanation.

Kim said meekly, "I can't do anything about the judging, I just knew I had to hit the best routines of my life, and I did that."[27]

Svetlana claimed that Kim did not have enough difficulty in her routines to be a World Champion and insinuated that Kim had won because the judges were biased in her favor. Was this true? On the next page is a comparison of the skills in Kim's routines versus those in Svetlana's.

KIM	SVETLANA
Vault:	**Vault:**
Full-twisting Yurchenko	Full-twisting Yurchenko
Bars:	**Bars:**
Gienger	Full Pirouette
Tkatchev	Tkatchev
Double Pike Flyaway	Double Pike Flyaway
Beam:	**Beam:**
Reverse Planche	Front Tuck Mount
B. Handspring-2 Layouts	B. Handspring-2 Layouts
Gainer Layout	Gainer Layout
Double Tuck Dismount	Double Tuck Dismount
Floor:	**Floor:**
Full-Twisting Double Pike	Full-Twisting Double Pike
3 Whips to Double Tuck	1½ twist to Double Tuck
Double Tuck Somersault	Double Pike Somersault

Both gymnasts had roughly equal levels of difficulty, except Kim performed two release moves on uneven bars and Svetlana only did one. Also, Kim's middle tumbling pass on floor was more complex. The only thing Svetlana had going for her was her front tuck beam mount, but that was comparable to Kim's reverse planche.

Svetlana's remark about Kim's level of difficulty was not valid. Svetlana's routines were, if anything, at a lower level than Kim's.

When asked about the criticism she had been receiving, Kim said, "[The controversy regarding the biased scoring] made me feel bad; it detracted some."[28]

* * *

The last competition of the World Championships was the event finals. The top eight finishers on each event after the team competition challenged for the gold on each apparatus. Kim qualified to two event finals: vault and floor exercise.

When asked about the pressure in the event finals, Kim said, "[There's] not actually any more pressure. I just wanted to go out and try my best."

Her first vault was uncharacteristically low, and she had to take a big lunge forward for a 9.75. Kim was not pleased. Her second vault, a handspring front, was only valued at a 9.90. She tucked her knees a little too soon on the horse and finished in a deep squat, and she had to take a step back. The judges gave her a 9.65.

In event finals, both vaults must be different and the scores are averaged. This is usually much harder for the gymnasts because they must hit both vaults, and one vault is typically much weaker because the athletes spend most of their time training the vault they use in team and all-around finals. Kim's average was a disappointing 9.70 for seventh place.

"It didn't go wonderful, but I'm not willing to trade in anything that happened from last night,"[29] she said.

In a controversial move, Kim refused to shake Svetlana's hand on the awards stand. Kim was hurt by the unfair comments Svetlana had made after the all-around final.

Kim also competed in the floor event finals. Julie Moran caught up with Mary Lou Retton before Kim's floor performance and asked if the American showing here was the beginning of the end of Soviet dominance in women's gymnastics. "I think so," grinned Mary Lou. "I think this competition, this World Championships, is an exact example of that. People are going to go to the Olympics next year and be afraid of the

Americans. It was always us going over there going, 'Oh my gosh, I wonder what the Soviets are doing.' Now they're going to be thinking, 'I wonder what the Americans are doing.' That's a huge breakthrough in American gymnastics."

Mary Lou said that Kim had worked hard as a youngster and now it was her time to shine. "She's going to have to have three solid tumbling passes" to win the gold on floor, Mary Lou remarked. "Now those are the guts of the routine because she can dance, and smile, and show her personality through her elements and her dance movements, but she's going to have to be really solid on her tumbling."[30]

In preparation for her floor routine, Kim mounted the podium. Svetlana coolly breezed by as she exited the apparatus, having just completed her unspectacular routine. Kim dazzled the crowd with an excellent routine identical to that of the all-around final. Bela gave her a big hug and lifted her up for the crowd to acknowledge. She seemed pleased, but it looked like her heavily bandaged left wrist was bothering her. She had been competing for several days, and the pressure and constant stress on her body was catching up with her. She scored a 9.95 to capture the bronze.

This time on the awards stand, Svetlana refused to shake Kim's hand to congratulate her. This was met by loud boos from the audience. Some bad blood seemed to be developing between these two gymnasts, making the coming clash in Barcelona all the more exciting.

Kim did not seem bothered by the handshake incident. "There's been some great gymnastics here, and handshakes aren't what we should be talking about,"[31] she said.

Julie Moran asked Kim and Bela if they had expected to win so many medals. Kim said, "Yeah, we had good preparation this summer, and we've competed against these people before, so it's no surprise."

Bela thought this was an important victory. "It is a strong message," he stated, "especially now in front of the summer Olympic Games, which is coming up in eleven months. That's a strong message, and I hope we establish ourself in the front of the international ranking as at least, you know, as powerful all-arounders and a very, very beautiful team."

Julie asked when Bela first thought Kim would be a star. He smiled and said, "She started to win about three years ago, and ever since she never gave up winning all-arounds, and she has several victories over the same people who we've been competing [against] tonight: the current, I mean, the former World Champion, Boginskaya, over Bontas, Milosovici, and all the other girls. So I was pretty confident she was gonna repeat her performances from the previous days."[32]

Apparently, television viewers preferred to watch Kim's first place all-around finish at the World Championships over Michael Jordan and the Chicago Bulls on NBC. ABC aired the Worlds February 29, 1992, five months after they had taken place, and they still produced a national rating of 5.3 to NBC's 4.7.[33]

The success of winning the 1991 World Championships brought Kim many awards and nominations. Kim and track and field champion Carl Lewis were voted United States Olympic Committee SportsWoman and SportsMan of the Year, respectively. At age fifteen, Kim was half of Carl Lewis's age and the first gymnast ever to win the award. She beat some other celebrities such as Jackie Joyner-Kersee, Summer Sanders, Tonya Harding, and Bonnie Blair.[34] She was also designated the March of Dimes Female Athlete of the Year and ABC *Wide World of Sports* Woman of the Year. Kim was again named one of the ten finalists for the 1991 Amateur Athletic Union's Sullivan Award, and she was nominated for the Associated Press Female Athlete of the Year.[35] She was also awarded the

Fédération Internationale de Gymnastique (FIG) insignia along with her teammates from the World Championships. A gymnast from any country who had averaged a 9.0 or higher in a World Championships or Olympic Games was given this honor.[36]

Kim had done something that no other American—male or female—had ever done: she had won the all-around title in a World Championships. Other marquis names in the sport, such as Olga, Nadia, and Mary Lou, had never held this title. This achievement would make Kim a legend in the sport.

"From that moment on, she was no longer just a person in the sport of gymnastics," Bela stated about Kim's victory. "Kim became a personality, an idol for millions of little girls, and an impressive part of U.S. gymnastics history."[37]

Chapter 6

SILENCING THE SKEPTICS

Kim decided to take the 1991-1992 school year off in order to train for the Olympics. This was her sophomore year of high school, and she did her school work through correspondence courses. It was good for her training because she could concentrate solely on gymnastics. However, she did not have much of a social life other than with her friends at the gym. She would have time for all of that after the Olympics, though.

"I don't have a very big social life right now, and I'm not going to school," Kim admitted. "My training is number one and whatever else doesn't fit in with it, I can't do it."[1]

Kim also did not have a boyfriend. "My male friends were never more than friends," Kim later disclosed. "With my training schedule, my time outside of the gym was limited. I was very determined to be the best gymnast that I could be, and I felt that it would be easier to stay focused on my goals without a boyfriend."[2]

Kim did get a break each week. She rested, relaxed, and spent time with family on Sundays, since that was the only day she did not have practice. Kim's closest friends were her younger sister, Melissa, and teammate Betty Okino. The three of them often spent Sunday afternoon bike-riding and hanging out together.

Kim's siblings were also involved in sports. Melissa played volleyball and swam for the school. Eric, Kim's brother, was a swimmer and played baseball and football.

Even with her rigorous schedule, Kim did not feel that she was missing out on her teenage life by spending so much time in the gym.

"It's not really that big of a sacrifice," she said, "because what I can get out of it and what I've already gotten out of doing gymnastics is totally worth it."[3] However, she said that "after [the Olympics in] 1992 I'd like to be a normal teenager."[4] She also joked that she would like to grow to six feet tall when she was finished with her gymnastics career, although she would settle for five.

Without the hindrance of school classes, Kim was able to put more emphasis on her workouts. Although she and Bela had not been getting along in the spring of 1991 because Bela had not liked her work habits, 1992 was a new year, and she had improved in this area.

Bela described Kim's new attitude: "With this new status [of World Champion], her mind is set. 'Yes, I have some obligations and I have to fulfill some other requirements which in the past, I did not consider so highly.'"

"I used to just be so-so in workout, and then I'd go in the competition and be able to do it, and everyone would [say] 'That's not fair,'" Kim laughed. "I think lately my workouts have been better, so hopefully that'll mean my competitions will be even better."[5]

Kim began the new year at the Alamo City Invitational on February 21-23, 1992 in San Antonio, Texas. In the team competition, Karolyi's A team easily defeated the rest of the field. It was really no contest, since three of the five members of the squad had competed on the 1991 World Championship silver medal team. Karolyi's A consisted of Kim, Hilary Grivich, Kerri Strug, Dominique Moceanu, and Jennie Thompson. In the all-around battle, Kim was able to successfully defend her title from the previous year, scoring 39 out of a possible 40 points. She also dominated in the event finals, winning on three of the four apparatuses: vault, floor exercise, and uneven bars (on which she scored a 10).[6]

The first major international competition of the Olympic year was the 1992 American Cup, which was held March 7 at the Orlando Arena in Orlando, Florida. Since Kim had won the World Championships, she felt added pressure to perform.

Although she thrived on pressure, Kim said that being cast as the favorite was "a little hard because a lot of people expect me to win, but I try to use that to my advantage, and I guess it's working." She continued, "I want to win everything I go into, that's what I'm training for. But now I feel like everyone else is saying, 'Well, she's supposed to win it,' too. It's like once you're up there, you don't want to lose because then everybody will look away and look at this other person."

Shannon Miller was struggling hard to be that "other person." She beat Kim in the preliminaries on every event except floor. But Kim was eager to win back the American Cup title she had lost last year to Betty Okino, who was not competing due to an injury.

Kim followed Shannon on all four of the events, which proved to be advantageous for Kim.

"I'm glad it was this way," she said about the competition order. "I got to know that I needed good routines on every event."

The first apparatus was the vault. Shannon nailed her full-twisting Yurchenko for a 9.95. Kim responded by sticking the same vault as Shannon for an even higher score of 9.987. Shannon then hit her bar routine for another 9.95, which Kim matched with a strong set of her own. After two rotations, Kim had a slight lead over Shannon.

Shannon was poised and ready to challenge for the lead on one of her best events, the balance beam. She had one of the hardest routines in the world and executed all her skills nicely: a back handspring to three layouts, back handspring whip, back handspring with a quarter twist, and a full-twisting double back dismount. She had a small hop on the dismount, but the outstanding difficulty she performed had to be considered when tallying her score. The judges awarded her a 9.95.

Kim was up next. As she was warming up her beam tumbling series on the mat, she almost hit Peggy Liddick, Shannon's beam coach, as Peggy walked over to congratulate Shannon on her fine beam routine. This incident did not affect Kim's concentration, however, and she confidently mounted and hit her reverse planche. Her tumbling series was perfect. Her full turn was flawless, and Bela mumbled "nice" and "good" after her leaps. She hit her new skill, back handspring whip, and Bela breathed a relieved "yes." This was the same element that had been a problem for her in the preliminaries.

The bell sounded as Kim prepared to dismount, letting her know she had ten seconds to get off the equipment. She landed well except for a small hop.

Bela gave her a big hug and patted her on the back, saying, "All right, Kimbo, good one." Kim received the same score as Shannon, a 9.95, to maintain her small lead.

Shannon's routine had a little more difficulty and both gymnasts had hops on the landing, but Kim was the defending

World Champion, and sometimes that played a part in receiving good scores. The judges recognized Kim and expected her routine to be superb, and when she did well she was rewarded. There were definite advantages to being "known" in the sport of gymnastics.

Kim's mother, Clarice, was happy that balance beam was over and that Kim had hit her routine. "I was sweating it after yesterday's [wobble on beam in the preliminaries]," she said. "It was pretty scary."

"She manages to block out everything and concentrate on what's beforehand and just does it," David Zmeskal said, recognizing his daughter's ability to handle pressure.

Clarice predicted that the meet would come down to the one who made the least mistakes. "I think they're both [Shannon and Kim] very strong," she said. "It's good to see that the United States has two good competitors like this."[7]

The final event was the floor exercise, Kim's strength. Shannon was first up and had problems in the touch warm-ups with her opening tumbling run. She had a pulled hamstring, which made it difficult to rotate her full-twisting double back far enough to land on her feet. Shannon looked troubled as she talked things over with her coach, Steve Nunno, before her routine.

The chimes sounded, marking the end of the warm-up period. Shannon walked gingerly out onto the floor as the crowd, seeing her worried expression, tried to encourage her. *"When the Saints Go Marching In"* began blaring over the loudspeakers, and Shannon began her routine. Unfortunately, she over-rotated her first tumbling run and fell out of bounds. She had over-corrected the problem she had been having in warm-ups. A noticeable grimace appeared on her face when she had to show a split; her injury was definitely hampering her performance.

Shannon had a low second pass and had to touch her hand to the floor. Her dance also reflected her grim mood. She successfully landed her final pass and limped over to her coaches looking like she would burst into tears.

"That's all right, you did a good job," consoled Steve Nunno. She scored a 9.212.

Meanwhile, on the other side of the arena, Bela gave Kim some last minute instructions. The announcer boomed her name over the loudspeakers as she raised her arms to the judges and to the zealous crowd, signaling that she was ready to go.

Unlike Shannon, Kim was able to fit her first pass, a whip back through to a full-twisting double pike somersault, in the allotted seventeen meters from one corner of the floor to the other. Bela's eyes watched Kim like a hawk, and he remarked "good" as she played to the crowd.

"Be careful," Bela warned as she started her second pass. She was again able to stay in bounds but did not quite finish the last flip of her double back somersault and had to take a noticeable step forward. Kim went all-out by ending with a very difficult full-twisting double pike somersault, the same skill she had previously used to open her routine.

Kim had upgraded her tumbling, although she could have won with a conservative routine because of Shannon's errors. It was a gutsy move that silenced many critics who claimed she did not have enough difficulty to be the World Champion.

After holding her ending pose for a moment, Kim ran off the mat and hugged Bela. She breathed a quick sigh of relief and waved to her adoring fans. The scoreboard flashed a 9.912, which put Kim's total score just shy of the record set the year prior by Betty Okino.

Kim regained the American Cup title she had lost in 1991, and Bela added another American Cup victory to his collection, bringing his grand total to ten. Henrietta Onodi placed second, and Shannon was third.

"I knew I had to do good routines every single time I went up," Kim remarked happily. "I'm very pleased with how I did."[8]

Prize money was again awarded to the top finishers, and Kim managed to take home $6,000 after her fine performance.

Randi Hall spoke with Kim about the neck-and-neck competition. "It was a very hard competition all the way through," Kim said. "Shannon and me were very, very close the whole competition. Kind of scary sometimes, but it pushed us to both do our best."

Randi asked Kim what she planned to do next. Kim smiled, "We're going to Disney World tomorrow and then we have McDonald's Mixed Pairs coming up next week."[9]

After a fun trip to Disney World, Kim participated in the 1992 McDonald's International Mixed Pairs meet on March 10 in Tallahassee, Florida. Again, she had to face Shannon Miller.

"This year we should be winning, and she wants to win," Steve Nunno bragged about his star pupil, Shannon. "We've been the person without the pressure. If you're going into the Olympic Games, you're not going to win unless you've won something. She's won a number of international competitions, and as I've said before, I think she's very well respected on the whole international scene. Unfortunately, she hasn't won a particular [major] meet in America . . . so it's our turn. She's got to earn it, she knows it, and we're ready for it."[10]

Kim was paired up with Jarrod Hanks who had won the 1992 men's American Cup title. Shannon Miller was matched with Scott Keswick.

Shannon went before Kim and elected to do the uneven bars. She performed a beautiful set with the tiniest hop on the landing for a 9.925. Her partner had an excellent still rings performance, giving them the lead after the first round.

Kim decided to begin on floor. She used her updated tumbling to impress the crowd at the Leon County Civic Center. She barely pulled her final pass around to her feet, but the judges liked the effort and gave her a 9.90. Jarrod also did floor exercise. He did very well, and Bela was quick to shake his hand to congratulate him. Their fine performances enabled them to advance to the next round tied for third place with the Russian pair of Svetlana Kozlova and Dmitri Karbonenko.

If the women were going to vault, they had to do it in the second round. Kim chose to vault because it was one of her strongest events. She ran hard, exploded off the board, and traveled a good distance from the vault but took a small hop on the landing. She received a 9.95.

Bela reminded her to concentrate on the landing. On her second attempt, she did almost the exact same vault and again had to take a hop. She scored another 9.95.

Bela patted Kim on the shoulders but did not give her the customary bear hug, which was reserved only for exceptional performances. He expected a lot from his pupils and had wanted Kim to score a 10. Since she had not, he seemed a little disappointed.

Jarrod mounted the still rings. He had a nice routine but bobbled on the landing for a 9.60. Although tied for third place with the Chinese pair, Kim and Jarrod could not advance due to the rule that only one American couple could compete in the final round.

Shannon Miller and Scott Keswick were in first place after two rotations and went on to win the competition. This was a great birthday present for Shannon, who turned fifteen on the day of the competition.

Kim returned home to Houston to train for awhile, then it was off to Los Angeles for Hilton's Superstars of Gymnastics. The exhibition was held March 28 at the Great Western Forum.

The greatest names in gymnastics were there and treated the crowd to a magnificent evening. Olga Korbut, Nadia Comaneci, and Mary Lou Retton performed routines, as did some members of the gold medal-winning 1984 United States men's Olympic team.

Sixteen-year-old Kim executed a near-perfect beam routine under the bright spotlights to the tune of *"You Are Everything"* sung by Rod Stewart. She smiled and waved to the crowd after her dismount as the flashes of many cameras lit her cheery face. Had this been a competition, she might have scored a 10, but there were no judges for exhibitions.

Kim closed the gymnastics reunion by displaying her award-winning floor exercise routine. She brought the house down with superb tumbling that made her look as if she had springs built into her legs. The crowd clapped and cheered to her upbeat music, and that seemed to give Kim a boost. She ended her routine with her trademark pose: lying with her back arched, both arms crossed in the air, one leg outstretched, and one leg bent. Kim waved with both hands to her countless fans and then ran off the mat.

After the exhibition, Kathy Johnson had a chance to interview Bela with his most famous trio of athletes: Nadia, Mary Lou, and Kim.

"Gosh," Bela exclaimed, "what can be more satisfying in the career of a coach than to see your star students together? And that's work of twenty-five years." He laughed. "Starting back in the older times in the '70s with Nadia, continuing with Mary Lou in '84, then right now with Kimbo going up into the fifth Olympic Games. That's a great moment, and I don't believe it can be more satisfying than this."

Kathy asked the three ladies about their idols. Nadia, whom one never thinks of as having an idol, said, "I had an idol, and my idol was [Ludmilla] Tourischeva, and I always dreamed to be like her . . . for me she looked great and everything she did was perfect."

Mary Lou said, "Nadia was my idol. I can remember back in '76 I was seven years old. I was laying on my stomach glued to the television watching her, and I said to my mother, 'Mommy, I want to be just like her,' and my mom patted me on the head and said, 'Sure, honey, sure.' She is the one that got me started. So it's nice to see that each generation has someone to look up to."

Kim's idol, of course, was Mary Lou, whom Kim had watched prepare for the 1984 Olympics. Kim said about her present company, "Well, it kind of makes me nervous sitting next to these two, but knowing that they put in their time and what they got out of it just pushes me to want to try even harder and hopefully repeat what they did." Kim continued, "It's kind of weird, because I never remember watching Mary Lou being unhappy or anything in the gym and I'm always like, 'How is this possible?'" She laughed shyly as her rosy cheeks glowed with embarrassment.

"I was [unhappy], Kim, several times," Mary Lou gushed. "I was just a good actress."[11]

* * *

Two weeks after the exhibition in Los Angeles, Kim jetted off to Paris, France, for the first Individual Apparatus World Championships ever held. Bela had debated whether or not to attend the meet but had finally decided to go.

"The competition did not fit into our preparation plan, but I still decided to go, recognizing the importance of the competition for the outcome of the Olympic Games," he said. "The world needed to see that Kim wasn't the World Champion because of the home-court advantage but her own skill and athletic prowess. In addition, I felt it was important to have one more successful European competition in a country next door to Barcelona—where the Games were to be held."[12]

The meet began on April 15. Each country was allowed to enter three gymnasts on each piece of equipment. There were three rounds of competition (preliminaries, semifinals, finals), and only two athletes per delegation were permitted in the final two rounds. Scores did not carry over from the previous day of competition.

Kim placed second in the preliminaries and fourth in the semifinals on balance beam. She had the disadvantage of going third in the finals; judges typically hold the higher scores for the last several athletes. Kim's scheme was to hit her set early and put the pressure on the remaining six gymnasts.

Kim mounted the beam and held her arched handstand with her feet hanging over her head and one knee bent so that one foot almost touched her ponytail. The cameras clicked furiously, but they did not seem to bother Kim. She stuck all of her layouts and sailed through the dismount, planting her feet firmly on the mat without any movement. She received a 9.925 and the early lead.

Kim sat back and watched several of the other gymnasts, including her adversary, Svetlana Boginskaya, wobble and crack under the stress. Kim was the only one to complete her routine with virtually no errors, and that earned her the gold.

Svetlana accepted Kim's victory and congratulated her on the awards stand by kissing both cheeks. Winning the balance beam proved it was no fluke that Kim had won the all-around in Indianapolis.

"It gives me a lot of confidence knowing that I can even win what's not even my best event," Kim said of her balance beam victory.

Kim won an apparatus gold medal, a feat that had not been

accomplished by a United States gymnast in a World Championships since Marcia Frederick's gold on uneven bars in 1978.

There were many falls in the beam event finals, possibly due to the rigorous schedule that the athletes had endured in order to keep advancing. Some gymnasts had gone to the gym early in the morning and had not finished until about midnight.

Regarding the falls, Kim said, "Luckily, I went up early enough in the rotation so I didn't have to watch everybody fall and think in the back of my mind that I could fall, too."

Several of the gymnasts complained about the quality of the balance beam. "It feels a little shaky," Kim admitted. "Today is the first day that I really felt comfortable on it."[13]

Kim tried for her second medal on floor exercise. She had won a bronze medal on floor at the 1991 World Championships in Indianapolis, and she was eager to prove her skeptics wrong by winning a gold medal outside of the United States.

Kim explained her reasons for wanting to compete in Paris: "I wanted to show the people I could . . . compete in Europe and also with more difficulty."[14]

Tatiana Lisenko, a prominent member of the Soviet team, had said in 1991, "If I were Kim Zmeskal, I would have made my routines a little more difficult. I think she can do this because she has a real fighting spirit."[15] Now, with an improved skill level, Kim was in search of another gold medal in a neutral setting.

In the preliminaries, Kim tied for second place with a 9.90. In the semifinals, she improved slightly with a 9.937 to capture the top spot.

Kim chose these World Championships to unveil her new floor routine that she would also use in the Olympics. Barry Nease had arranged Kim's new routine, this time to the fun tune of *"Rock Around the Clock."* Geza Pozsar, who owned a gym and coached in California, again did the choreography.

113

Geza visited every few weeks to make little changes and sharpen Kim's dance movements. He helped throughout the year and more frequently as the Olympics approached. There were also several dance teachers at Bela's gym who worked with Kim on a daily basis.

The crowd at the Palais Omnisport began to clap immediately as Kim snapped her fingers and swung her arms to the music. She used her difficult tumbling—whip to a full-in, three whips to a double back, and a full-in—to make a statement that she definitely deserved to be the World Champion, and she was going to prove it. Her playful motions, waving and clapping to the audience during her routine, garnered loud applause. Kim was the favorite here, and the crowd loved her. She waved her hands and then jogged toward Bela to catch his reaction to her exciting new routine. He gave her a big hug as her score, 9.937, was flashed.

Kim seemed a little disappointed, but Bela reassured her, shaking his head and saying, "You don't have to worry."

Henrietta Onodi, whom Kim bumped out of first place, walked over to give Kim a congratulatory hug. She later admitted that she thought Kim's floor routine was better than hers that day.

Kim was the only gymnast to end her floor routine with a very difficult full-twisting double pike somersault. This all-out performance confirmed her number-one world ranking and intensified some rivalries between Kim and the Eastern Bloc gymnasts.

Interestingly, Svetlana Boginskaya decided not to compete in floor exercise. She did not want to unveil her new floor routine until the Olympics in Barcelona.

For the second time that week, Kim got to hear her national anthem played before the large crowd.

Kathy Johnson asked Kim after the meet if this win sent a

message to the gymnastics community and her critics. Kim nodded and replied, "Yes, because a lot of people were criticizing me that I only won [the World all-around title] because I was in the U.S. and that my tumbling was not strong enough to get a bronze on floor. I upgraded my tumbling and won a gold here, so I'm real happy."[16]

Bela gave his view of the competition: "It was a very difficult competition where you had to perform three days in a row to be in the top. Kim is still the strongest all-around and consistent athlete in the world."[17]

After all of her successes and gold medal performances, Kim said, "I still picture myself sort of as that little eight-year-old looking up to Mary Lou." She found it hard to believe that she was the one in the spotlight. "It doesn't seem like other people would do that to me." Kim smiled and bit her lip, "Maybe they do."[18]

Kim was on a roll. She had not lost a meet since the 1991 American Cup. Her relationship with Bela was back on track. Her future seemed bright. She was at the top of her game heading into the Olympic team selection. It seemed like Kim would breeze through the Olympic Trials and easily walk away with the number-one ranking going into Barcelona.

Kim seemed invincible. What could go wrong now?

Chapter 7

MAKING THE DREAM TEAM

After her two gold medal-winning triumphs at the Individual Apparatus World Championships in Paris, Kim had a brief one-month break from competition to train in Houston, then it was off to the 1992 Phar-Mor U.S. Championships held May 14-17. Kim made the journey to Columbus, Ohio, to defend her two previous U.S. Champion titles. The competition would not be as fierce as usual, since Betty Okino and Shannon Miller would not be competing because of injuries.

The U.S. Championships were a very important part of the United States Olympic team selection process. This meet and the Olympic Trials would decide the top eight spots. Eventually, the team would be narrowed down to six. The top twelve finishers from the Championships would advance to the Olympic Trials. Sixty percent of the compulsory score and 40 percent of the optional score would be tallied to determine the placements.

Shannon defeated Kim in the compulsories but was unable to participate in the optional round since she was still rehabilitating her elbow from recent surgery. Betty did not even travel to the competition because of her injuries.

The fear of injuries was something shared by most gymnasts, especially close to the Olympics. Kim said solemnly, "I feel scared for her [Betty] because I know how much work she's put into it. And also I'm scared for myself because it could happen to anyone. Injuries happen; a lot of times there is nothing you can do about it. I'm just praying for Betty and praying for everybody else that they can get through this."

Shannon and Betty would still get a chance to compete in the Olympic Trials. The United States Gymnastics Federation allowed them to petition directly through to the Trials because they had been key members of the U.S. team in past major international competitions, such as the World Championships.

"I hope that they'll be ready for the next competition, because we'll really need them in Barcelona," Kim said of Betty and Shannon.

The pressure was great at the Championships. "You can kind of feel it," Kim said. "I think everybody sorta can in here—that they know that what they do here will contribute to making the team."[1]

With Shannon dropping out of the competition, Kim was in first place. She began the optional round on the vault. Bela gave her some final hand signals that looked like a secret code only Kim could decipher and use to improve her vault.

On her first attempt, Kim ran down the runway with her lips pressed firmly together and determination blazing in her eyes. Her eighty-pound frame soared through the air and landed without error. Kim thrust her arms high above her head to complete the movement.

"That was a good one," Bela laughed.

The judges agreed. They gave her a 10.

On her second try, Kim did a carbon copy of the first vault.

"That was a good one," Bela said again, slapping her on the back.

The judges gave her another 10.

"It was a great way to start the competition,"[2] Kim admitted.

She followed her perfect vaults with an outstanding uneven bar set. She seemed to float above the bar during her release moves. Her only visible error was a slight shuffle on the landing.

Bela thought the routine was satisfactory and patted Kim on the back. However, she scored a 9.675. Bela was not pleased with the judges' decision.

"That can't happen here in the Championship now!" he yelled angrily as he rushed over to the score table to protest Kim's low mark. "Then to hell with it!" Filled with rage, Bela indicated to the judges that if they did not improve their marks, he would pull his athletes out of the meet.

Bela then told Mike Jacki, the executive director of the USGF, that Kim's score was improper given her World Champion status. He filed a protest to request the specific deductions and asked if the scores could be raised for both Kim and Kerri Strug on uneven bars.

"Well, we came here to the Championship of the United States to first of all honor our National Championships," Bela later explained. "Unfortunately, we got into the sorriest situation I've ever been in my life." He could not believe the scores his team was receiving from, as he described, "a bunch of incompetent, totally out of their mind, I would say, not judges." He continued, "The first event was the only satisfaction when the scores settled in the normal range, and immediately after that [they went] totally wild. Wild out of any kind of order, out of any kind of control. I believe those people have no idea what they are doing. They have no knowledge of what causes gymnastics expertise and overall I think just a sorry bunch."[3]

Typically, the scores at the U.S. Championships were lower than in other competitions, and this frustrated Bela. He had experienced a similar disagreement the previous year during the compulsory competition and had almost been ejected from the meet.

Meanwhile, Kim and Kerri tried to stay focused and warmed-up their balance beam routines on the sidelines.

Kim did not involve herself in the politics of the sport. "I just let all the politics stuff up to Bela and the judges and whatever, because I'm in gymnastics because I love it, and that's why I started and that's why I'm still doing it," she said with a smile. "I love to compete. I don't really have anything to say about who's going to win and who's going to get each score, so I just do my job and leave all the rest to the people who make those decisions."[4]

The reigning World Champion on balance beam, Kim made the apparatus look like a wide table instead of a four-inch piece of wood. She did a nearly flawless routine and was welcomed with a big hug from Martha. Because of her ability to concentrate, Kim rarely fell off balance beam or any other piece of equipment during competition.

Kim moved to her final event, the floor exercise, as the leader. She began her routine with a very high full-twisting double back, but she landed with her left foot on the white boundary line, resulting in an automatic one-tenth penalty. The rest of her tumbling was perfect, and the crowd at the St. John Arena clapped wildly.

"That was a big one," Bela remarked to Kim regarding the

119

height of her opening pass. He hugged her and added matter-of-factly, "Yeah, you did step out [of bounds]."

The judges suspiciously overruled the out-of-bounds deduction, which raised a few eyebrows from the other coaches. Kim scored a 9.90 to win her third national title, an accomplishment that had not been duplicated for eighteen years. The only other female gymnast to win three or more national titles was Joan Moore Rice, who had captured four consecutive victories from 1971-74. Kim also set a new all-around record with 78.59 points.

Kerri Strug placed second and conceded, "Kim is the World Champion, and to be second to her is great."[5]

In the event finals, Kim dominated by winning balance beam and floor exercise while placing second on vault and uneven bars.

After the meet, Kim critiqued her own performance by saying, "My events felt pretty strong. [I made] a couple mistakes, but there is a couple more meets, and that's what I'm looking for."

When asked, Kim was reluctant to disclose changes to her routine for the Olympic Trials. "I'm not real sure," she said. "We still have a couple more weeks."[6] She had been wanting to add a double layout to her floor routine for quite some time. She was hoping the Olympic Trials would be the place to do it.

Bela was still upset about the scoring. "To try to discredit Kim two months before the Olympic Games was stupid and unbelievably cruel," he claimed, angry with the judges. "She wasn't just a person in gymnastics, she was a personality who elevated the whole sport of American gymnastics. She should have been protected, cherished, and preserved."[7]

After the Phar-Mor U.S. Championships, a banquet was held at which the best athletes and coaches of the year were selected. Kim won the Women's Athlete of the Year, and Bela won the Women's Coach of the Year.

* * *

Kim went back to Houston for a month of intense training before the Olympic Trials. With the Olympics so close, the training was very difficult and demanding. Kim and her teammates began at 7:00 in the morning and ended about 11:00, then they returned at 5:30 p.m. and worked until 9:00 in the evening.

In an average morning workout, Kim stretched out and performed light tumbling, then she ran for thirty minutes, sometimes turning to go backwards, then sideways, then lifting her knees up as high as possible. There was no talking, laughing, or music allowed.

"Oh, no way," Kim said, in mock terror.

The first part was just a warm-up. The real workout began with six or seven compulsory uneven bar and balance beam routines, two compulsory floor routines, and many, many compulsory vaults. That is, *if* she was hitting them. If Kim was having problems, she had to do more routines until her coaches were satisfied.

Bela could be heard barking, "Harder, harder," during the tumbling exercises. Once in awhile, Bela complimented someone with a "Good," but most of the time he called out, "What are you doing?" or "Is no good! Do it right!"

And then there was conditioning. Kim conditioned for half an hour to an hour, and sometimes more. She did hundreds of sit-ups, push-ups, V-ups, leg lifts, pull-ups on a bar, and more sit-ups hanging from a bar to maintain strength. Kim's workout also included aerobics to give her stamina.[8]

In the evening, Kim returned to complete six or seven optional uneven bar and balance beam routines, and two full optional floor routines. The same rule applied as in the morning: if the routines were good, she would not have to do as many. Vaulting was done until Bela felt Kim had done an adequate amount. Optionals involved more difficult skills and took more endurance to perform.

Bela encouraged parents to stay and watch their children practice. Onlookers sat in the front room and peered through the glass while their children worked harder than most professional athletes.

"He's very intense with the kids," Clarice Zmeskal said, describing Bela during practice. "He wants them to be perfect all the time, even in everyday workout."[9] She continued, "He does the coaching; we do the parenting. But sometimes it is hard to take."

Bela described his attitude in the gym: "We are not in the gym to be having fun. The fun comes in the end, with the winning and the medals." He shook his clenched fist and declared, "Sometimes the preparation is so hard, so intense. They are crying, they are screaming. It is over the top."[10]

To put it simply, Bela said, "My attitude is never to be satisfied, never enough. The girls must be little tigers, clawing, kicking, biting, roaring to the top. They stop for one minute—poof!—they are finished."[11]

After the grueling training sessions, Bela's kids were in top form and ready to make a statement at the Trials. He had three tough kids who went to the Trials: Kim, Kerri Strug, and Hilary Grivich. Each was determined to make the team.

The Olympic Trials, some thought, were more nervewracking than the actual Olympics. But Kim could handle the situation, Bela said, because she had nerves of steel and was better able to deal with pressure than any other gymnast he had coached.

"She is a fierce competitor," Bela said. "She is a very

strong, a very aggressive, a very stable, and a very balanced competitor. Overall, I would say probably one of the strongest competitors I had in my thirty years of coaching career."

Mary Lou agreed. "She handles pressure better than anybody I've ever seen," she marveled. "Really and truly, she is a competitor."[12]

Kim put it simply: "I like competitions. I like winning. I guess that's pretty much me."[13]

Kim wanted to use all the pressure that came with the attention she had been receiving to enhance her performance.

"I feel like a lot more people are watching, and a lot more people are concerned about how I'm doing," she said. "It's a little extra pressure, but I usually do better under pressure anyway, so I guess that is to my advantage."

The media began bombarding Kim with questions about the 1992 Olympics immediately after she arrived in Baltimore for the Trials.

"I like the attention; sometimes it gets a little much when I'm trying to train," Kim admitted. "But I guess that's what comes with it. Our sport needs more media promotions."

The media did not seem concerned with Kim making the Olympic team—her reason for being in Baltimore. Instead, they wanted to talk about the U.S. medal possibilities at the Olympics.

Kim reminded them that the Olympic team had not yet been chosen: "People are saying things about what I'm going to do in Barcelona. It's like, we still have the Trials, nobody is definitely on there, anything can happen."[14]

The Trials were held June 11-13, 1992. Shannon Miller again placed ahead of Kim after the compulsories.

"I had a few minor breaks in my routines," Kim said, attributing them to her nervousness. "You don't want to mess up on what is supposedly the 'easy' things."[15]

Shannon's coach, Steve Nunno, was hoping that his star athlete would give Kim a good fight. "Beating Kim Zmeskal, the World Champion, would be a tremendous feat for Shannon," he said. "I don't think that Shannon has ever lost to Kim, necessarily; Shannon has beaten herself every time we've been on the floor."[16]

The competition began on vault. During the warm-up period, both Kim and Shannon looked sharp. But when the competition began, Shannon seemed a little unsure of herself and performed two vaults that were much lower than usual and not as crisp, opening the door for Kim.

Kim stepped up to her starting marker confidently, stuck both arms out to the side and glared down the runway. She sprinted toward the vault and hit the springboard just right to propel herself high in the air. She opened up into a nice arch and firmly planted the landing.

The vault was perfect. Bela raised his arms and threw his head back triumphantly.

Kim was not satisfied, though. She walked toward Bela and said plainly, "It could be higher." He agreed and gave her some pointers.

Meanwhile, the crowd at the Baltimore Arena went crazy as the judges posted a 10, the fifth perfect vault of Kim's career. But Kim showed no emotion and concentrated on her second attempt. She duplicated her first vault and received a second 10, just as she had done at the Nationals a month ago.

Next was uneven bars, Shannon's best event. She added a third release move to her already difficult set and earned a 9.937. Kim definitely had her work cut out for her.

Kim started with a Gienger that had ample height, but as she swung over the low bar, her right hand failed to grasp it properly and her forearm banged the bar. She kept the momentum going, though, and completed her second release move. Then she stuck the dismount.

Bela gave Kim a big hug. After a brief judges' conference she was awarded a 9.812. In a familiar scenario, Bela was extremely unhappy with the score and filed a protest.

Many people had accused Bela of being outspoken and trying to intimidate the judges, a charge to which he responded with an emphatic, "Bah!" He explained: "You have to have competent people evaluating the athlete, not the housewives! It is ridiculous in a civilized country that the finest athletes, who have spent years—most of their lives preparing for, in many cases, a single Olympic Games—athletes who are prepared by professionals at the highest level, are evaluated by housewives who were not gymnasts, who are not coaches, who in some cases—they know who they are—are in the employ of the clubs they judge. Housewives, you know, who do not spend time in the gym. These are the people who in the USA are responsible for placing our athletes. They are incompetent and it is an insane system that keeps these people in a position of power."

Bela continued, "One more thing along with competence is the issue of personal bias. I am angry and I am often vocal. Now, if you are jealous of me or dislike me, okay. That is between you and me. Come hit me, or—ptooey!—spit at me, but don't retaliate by giving bad scores. Do not hurt the athlete; that is wrong. What can we do? Put competent people in charge like is done internationally."

Bela suggested one way the system could be improved: "Coaches and former gymnasts need to be out on the floor judging the gymnasts. A former gymnast, someone who has been there and who can look through the eyes of the athlete, needs to be evaluating. How can someone who has not been a gymnast, and who is never in the gym and who only knows gymnastics by judging in meets, truly understand the sport and evaluate placing for the athletes?"

Kim, as usual, did not concern herself with the discrepancies between the judges and Bela. She was second to compete on the balance beam, which was not advantageous because the scores could possibly be higher for the later gymnasts. But she did not let that bother her, either.

Kim seemed anxious to begin, and with her hands on her hips she said, "Okay, let's go," while waiting for the first person to start after the warm-up period had ended.

Kim was able to stay on the beam during her two layouts, but she had an uncharacteristic wobble. Her layouts had been problematic in warm-ups, so it was good that she was able to at least stay on the beam. She had another major wobble on her full turn, and her second tumbling series was average. She completed her mediocre performance with a hop on the dismount.

Kim did not smile as she saluted the judges. Wiping her brow and hanging her head, she walked toward Bela. He patted her on the shoulders and looked displeased as he shook his head negatively.

"I guess I wasn't straight,"[17] said a dazed Kim, referring to her mistake on the layout.

Martha talked with Kim about the errors, and when she was finished, Bela tried to prepare her for the next event. He shook her shoulders gently and she looked up at him with watery eyes and a worried expression. Her score, 9.737, was announced, and she tried to forget about her less-than-stellar beam set and get mentally psyched-up for floor exercise.

Shannon, meanwhile, hit her very difficult beam routine. She had one wobble and a step on the landing for a 9.90. On floor, Shannon used a new classical routine set to Hungarian Gypsy violin music. She turned in another excellent performance to score a 9.762.

Kim's big blue eyes bore a look of deep concentration as she stepped onto the floor mat. She warmed up a beautiful double layout somersault, which would definitely make her routine the most difficult of the competition.

As her music began, Kim was off with a whirl. Her whip back to double layout, which was so high it seemed in the rafters, was perfect. She hopped, smiled, clapped, and waved to the crowd during her routine. Her middle pass of three whip backs to a double back somersault received deafening applause from the capacity crowd who had paid $50.00 for an average seat. To top it all off, Kim nailed her full-twisting double pike somersault—the same pass most gymnasts used to begin their routines—to bring the house down.

Bela and Martha rushed to congratulate Kim. This was probably the best and most difficult floor routine of Kim's career. Unfortunately, the judges did not recognize the perfection of the routine and gave her only a 9.95. The scores were lower than normal on this event as a whole. Bela was again dissatisfied with the score and wanted a 10 from the judges.

There was much controversy over deciding the actual winner of the meet and choosing the top six team members. Adding up the scores from compulsories and optionals, Kim beat Shannon at the Olympic Trials. Kim had a total of 79.048 and Shannon's total was 79.010. However, in the Trials, 60 percent of the compulsory score was combined with 40 percent of the optional score to get the final results. By this method, Kim outscored Shannon by one thousandth (.001) of a point. However, the final tally was calculated using the weighted scores from *both* the U.S. Championships and the Olympic Trials. The Championship totals counted for 30 percent and the totals from the Trials counted for 70 percent to select the privileged six. By this scoring, Shannon won (although her weighted score from the Trials counted 100 percent because she did not complete the U.S. Championships competition). Shannon scored 79.056 and Kim scored 78.916.

This overly-complex method of selecting the six team members was very confusing. Besides, Shannon had only competed in one of the two meets, and comparing her one score with Kim's scores from both meets was like comparing apples to oranges. It just did not work!

There was a clear battle developing between Bela and Steve Nunno over which American gymnast was better and should merit the number-one ranking going to Barcelona. Despite their coaches, Kim and Shannon were friends.

"The [World] Champion deserves to get some credit," Steve said about Kim. "[But] Shannon's time was going to come. People knew it. And it's starting to come now."

Bela was very upset. He felt that Kim had been penalized for competing in both meets, even though she scored the most points.

Steve said of the top two American gymnasts, "I realized Kim and Shannon, at some point, were going to be a controversial issue. They were two great competitors. Shannon wanted it. I wanted it. Kim wanted it. Bela wanted it."

Bela agreed: "No doubt about it. It's a rivalry." But he knew the important number-one ranking going into Barcelona was secondary to the team competing at its utmost ability, so he shifted his attention, stating, "That's the main thing now, lining them up side by side and getting the best out of them."[18]

Kim seemed to have the right perspective, saying, "I made some mistakes and it came out in the end. My placement is not as important as correcting my mistakes for the next meet. None of this is going to matter in a month. What people are going to remember is who won the Olympics, not who won the Olympic Trials."

Bela was not happy with the team selection process, and when he was asked to be the Olympic coach he said, "I won't accept it. Who is going to take this responsibility? Who is going to work this out without raising the biggest [questions]? Not for me. They [the USGF] like these muddy waters. The better to hide, the better to fish in."

Despite the minor feud between the coaches, Kim was enjoying her status as an Olympic team member. There were neat perks associated with being on the team, like all the attention and free merchandise from sponsors. Kim loaded up on goodies, including Ray-Ban sunglasses and a Cabbage Patch Kid. The doll was the team mascot, and several of the dolls were provided to be given to children at Barcelona hospitals.

Kim was also invited to the United States Olympic Training Center (USOC) in Colorado Springs, Colorado, for the unveiling of a hairstyling salon on the campus for athletes to use while training at the center. Kim helped USOC President William Hybl cut the tape in the opening ceremony. Supercuts also styled Kim's hair and gave her a makeover.

"It is very important that you feel good about how you look when you are competing, and Supercuts is here to help all these athletes accomplish that,"[19] she said.

Kim and her teammates returned to Houston to train fervently at Bela's ranch for three weeks. This would be their last training time at home before the Olympics. Bela wanted his gymnasts to be completely ready for Barcelona.

Bela said of his preparation strategy, "I push myself probably over any kind of limits and, of course, not just providing the coaching performance but providing everything, whatever you could strengthen my athletes' performances: conditions, athletic conditions, that motivational part, which I so specifically want them to change the attitude to make them winning athletes—stepping on the floor, wanting to win, having the pleasure and having the satisfaction. 'Yes, we are the best. We came here to win. Let's see who's around.' You know, just like back in the old times."[20]

The top seven from the Olympic Trials plus Betty Okino were invited to participate in a training camp in Orlando, Florida, on July 7-9. Because of an elbow injury, Michelle Campi did not participate in the Trials but used 100 percent of her score from Nationals to place in the top seven.

After the training session, a mock meet was held where the gymnasts performed their compulsory routines in the morning and their optional routines in the evening for each of the events. Brown's Gymnastics was the site of these trials, which were closed to the public.

A committee consisting of the eight gymnasts' coaches and one USGF official was established to select the seven gymnasts who would go to Barcelona. They met late into the night to vote on which of the eight girls would be cut from the team, and Kim Kelly ended up as the odd person out.

This process caused much debate, since the Olympic Trials did not really select the final women's team. Rather, the coaches themselves did. Even at this point, the team was not finalized since one more athlete needed to be cut in Barcelona. Only six gymnasts were allowed on the team.

Bela defended his position on removing Kim Kelly, indicating that it was fair and done by the rules. "I guarantee to everybody, only one reason was behind the decision: to select the best team to represent the United States of America in the Olympic Games,"[21] he said.

Kim agreed for the most part with the team selection. "I really believe that the two athletes that were missing from the Trials [Betty Okino and Michelle Campi] belonged on the team talent-wise and what they'd already shown in international competition," she said. However, she still saw room for improvement in the way the team was formed. "There really needs to be some sort of trial or, 'This is the trial for the team,' and then after that, that's all."[22]

The seven lucky women—Kim, Shannon Miller, Betty Okino, Kerri Strug, Dominique Dawes, Michelle Campi, and Wendy Bruce—made the training squad that left on Sunday, July 12 for France. There, the final alternate was to be decided. Many on the team had dedicated their lives and trained eight hours a day, six days a week just for the chance to go to the Olympic Games.

Unfortunately, Kim hurt her left leg while practicing in France. As a result, she was having difficulty in training, especially on floor exercise. She had also been suffering from a stress fracture in her left wrist which had not healed in over a year. Kim was frustrated. She did not want to see her Olympic dream slip away because of an injury she could not control.

Once they arrived in Barcelona, the media noticed that Kim had removed some elements from her floor exercise. John Tesh and Bob Costas of NBC questioned Bela about Kim's caution.

"She will put back everything when the competition starts," Bela stated. "We did protect a little bit the sore area and did not want to expose her for any kind of additional damage which might be collected through excessive usage through the full routine. Wasn't anything important for us. The podium training was a great checkup of the kids, of the possibilities, and spatially the equipment. So she will up with the full routines."

Bela spoke of the injury as if it was no big deal. He did not want the press focusing on it or bothering Kim about it. The truth was that she had developed a nasty stress fracture in her left leg. The pain was incredible, but she was not willing to give up because she had worked ten long years for this chance. Nothing was going to stop her, not even unbearable pain.

Bela was interviewed by NBC, the network covering the Olympics, shortly before the women's competition began. He was asked about the United States' medal possibilities.

Having seen the Unified and Romanian teams practice, he responded, "I certainly feel optimistic. The kids are prepared and they are ready to show off their capabilities and their willingness to win. And I hope after those many years that we might get the chance one more time to roll over the Soviets before they fall apart."

This would be Bela's last duel with the Soviets, now called the Unified team, since their empire and reign in gymnastics was about to be dismantled. Bela still had some built-up hostility and dislike for them, which was evident when he shared his feelings about them.

"In my mind, they are still the ultimate monster machine which was rolling over many, many years over small countries with modest possibilities and not giving us a chance to shine and really bring up the best from our sport," Bela said. "Of course, this rivalry is long lasting, back started in '72 and ever since is rolling, rolling through the Olympic Games."

Bela remembered the biased 1980 Olympics in Moscow. "I really got a lot of bad, not just publicity, but a lot of backlash from our [Romanian] government which later on considered a tremendous political mistake what I did over there, protesting for the rights of our kids," he explained. "But that was the Russian monster machine, the communist machine rolled over no matter young kids, young feelings, hurting everybody. The only goal they have is win, win, and win. I accept the winning but in a fair way."[23]

The final U.S. team was selected the day before the competition. Because of an injury, Michelle Campi became the alternate.

Bela was happy with the end results. "This is gonna be our best team ever," he exclaimed. "This is gonna be it!"[24]

The women's team selection process received much criticism. The team had been decided after several grueling meets. First there had been the U.S. Championships, then the Olympic Trials, then the private meet in Orlando, and finally the training sessions in France. The athletes had been required to constantly be at their best, because it had never seemed that they were definitely on the team. It was hoped that the torturous selection process could be put aside and the one-day-old team would pull together to turn in the best performance to date for the United States in an Olympics.

Kim shared her opinion of the team selection process: "It was a little bit long and dragged out, and it sort of made it hard for us to concentrate on our real goal, which was to do our best in the Olympic Games. And we sort of had to prove ourselves like five or six times, and it sort of gets to you after a while."[25]

Kim suggested some improvements and new ideas for the next Trials: "I think maybe, if anything, they should make it [the Trials] a little bit closer to the Olympics, but the athletes trying for the team shouldn't have to keep re-qualifying. We thought after Trials that we were on the team. And then like every workout seemed to us like we had to keep proving ourselves to everyone instead of being able to focus on the goal, which was to do our best at the Olympics, instead of every day being almost scared to mess up. With training, it's going to happen sometimes, but you almost felt like you weren't allowed to make any mistakes."[26]

"It is great dilemma having the system that picks best six or seven athletes to compete," Bela said. "If you pick them too early and you can't train them together, then it is a problem with fitness. The system should be able to pick the top seven, not three or four or five of seven. If they are not the best seven, then the selection system is wrong." Bela added, "You need flexibility, and a group of at least eight to be in full preparation. A final trials is good if the athletes have had the opportunity to train and pull together as a team. There are many pressures."[27]

Perhaps the most devastating thing that resulted from the team selection process was that the gymnasts started questioning themselves, becoming uncertain of their value as individual contributors. Doubt began to seep into their minds.

"Kim Zmeskal's spirit was systematically broken," Bela reflected bitterly about the entire process once the Olympics were concluded. "It began with the Nationals. I could see it in her eyes; they were wide open, trying to understand some of the judges. I could see that her mind was full of confusion: 'Am I the one who is supposed to be appreciated? Or, am I a public enemy? Who am I? What is this situation? What is going on here? Why do these people hate me?' Kim had just won the World Championship; she had the right to expect appreciation. All I could say to Kimbo throughout the whole mess was, 'Be strong.' But that wasn't enough. She wasn't one to be fooled by a pat on the back. She knew what was going on, and she knew it would only get worse."[28]

Chapter 8

THE FALL

Everyone was proclaiming Kim the one to beat in Barcelona. She appeared on NBC's *Today* show after the Olympic Trials. Shannon Miller was also supposed to appear, but according to Steve Nunno, Bela must have bumped her off the show. Before the Olympic Games, Kim was pictured on the cover of *TV Guide* and *Time* magazine. NBC heaped more pressure on Kim with a little promotion spot saying she was the one to watch. In addition, HBO did a feature on Kim several months before the Olympics showing highlights of her career and touting her as America's best hope.

Kim felt the pressure from all this media attention. "It's a little harder in some ways, that I have extra pressure on me," she said. "A lot more people expect more from me, but on the other hand it should be an advantage for me to go into the competition and know that people already notice me before I do anything."

"With the visibility and with this public popularity comes the pressure which is mounting over the person who is handling it," Bela said of Kim's popularity. "Of course, the great predecessors of her, Nadia and Mary Lou, haven't had to go through this pretty tough competitive time. Some days I would call a nightmare when everybody jumps on you expecting you to pose in a position which you are not yet, as an Olympic Champion."[1]

Realizing that most of the attention since the World Championships had been focused solely on her, Kim graciously said, "I felt like it wasn't fair, because the whole team did so well in Indianapolis that we should have all been able to get more of that with the media."[2]

Even Nadia Comaneci thought Kim would win. Nadia spoke very highly of Kim and her teammates.

"I was good at my time, but they are unbelievably good now," she said. "The difficulty is very high and there are lots of great gymnasts today. One of them, the World Champion, Kim Zmeskal, is an American who is coached by my former coach, Bela Karolyi. I believe she will be [the champion] in 1992, because I not only believe in her but I believe a lot in Bela. Everything he is touching, he is like doing miracles."[3]

Mary Lou shared a little different impression of Kim: "She makes me nervous when I watch her compete. Kim doesn't show any kind of emotion."

Kim had a lively personality which came through on floor exercise, but on the other events she wore an expressionless stare and turned intensely quiet, focusing on the job at hand.

Kim did not want people to mistake her game face for shyness. "I'm not quiet,"[4] she insisted.

Although everyone expected her to win, Kim tried to keep her head straight. "I personally knew that I was definitely not just going to go there and anything was going to be easy," she said. "I've never felt like that for any competition. I go into a competition, and I can remember always looking at the competitors, going, 'Wow, she's really great, she's really great also . . . I hope I can still stay with the competition.'"[5]

But Kim did not want to disappoint her fans. One thing was for sure: she would try to her fullest potential to bring home a gold medal.

"I like to compete in everything I do. I don't like to do things unless I can win them,"[6] she stated. "I've been working ten years for this goal and it's so close now it's almost frightening. I've been looking for the year 1992 to come around for a very long time. It's here and it's going."[7]

Kim dreamed of what the Olympics would be like. "I imagine it being really bright," she said pensively. "I'm like this little person, and the whole world is watching. I'm just doing my thing, pulling it off."[8]

Her dreams were becoming reality. It was time to begin the most difficult competition she would ever experience. The ten years of intense preparation were about to be put to the test.

* * *

Kim's first day of competition in the 1992 Summer Olympic Games was on Sunday, July 26. It was the team compulsories.

The United States had a good draw in the compulsories; none of the American gymnasts had to compete in the generally lower-scoring first round. Dominique Dawes and Wendy Bruce were designated to start in the second round, and they got the ball rolling with good performances.

Kerri Strug and Betty Okino continued the momentum in the third round and managed to narrow the lead of the Unified team and Romania.

The best were saved for last. Kim and Shannon Miller competed in the fourth and final round.

Kim began on beam with a steady press to a handstand. The compulsory beam routine was not difficult. She knew that she just needed to be steady. Good compulsory scores would help the team and help her qualify for the all-around finals. There she would fight to win the gold, to realize her lifelong dream.

Kim skipped to the end of the beam, turned, and paused. Everything was going fine. The tiny girl of long ago whom Bela had once described as "legendary for her falls . . . like popcorn popping on and off" seemed but a distant memory at this moment. The gymnast up there now was Kim Zmeskal the World Champion, legendary not for her falls but for her steadiness and strength. For her poise and skill and her silent determination.

Kim raised her arms and looked down the length of the narrow beam. She had practiced this a thousand times before: cartwheel to a back handspring to a split jump. It was at times like these when it seemed the endless repetitions Bela had forced her to do would pay off.

Then disaster struck.

The cartwheel was all right, but the back handspring was way off to the side. Her upper body shifted to the left and her right leg went up as she tried to regain her balance. She clutched desperately at the air.

For a brief moment that will always be etched upon her mind, she balanced there precariously.

Then she fell.

Kim's first thought when she jumped back up on the beam was, "I didn't fall."[9]

Because of the error, Kim was unable to connect the split jump to the back handspring, which would result in an additional deduction besides the automatic five-tenth penalty for the fall.

Kim continued the routine with a dazed look on her face. She finished the exercise without any other errors and saluted the judges.

Kim walked toward Bela feeling stunned and numb. She wiped her forehead and looked at him in despair. He tried to keep her spirits up and told her she still needed to do good routines on the next events.

"There's nothing lost yet," Bela encouraged. "Go for it!"[10]

A 9.35 was posted. Kim's score did not count for the team total because she had the lowest score on beam, and the lowest score on each event in compulsories and optionals was thrown out.

On the other side of the arena, Shannon Miller began her uneven bar routine. She nailed it, scoring a 9.912.

Kim tried to stay focused and not dwell too much on her previous routine by stretching out for floor exercise. She did over-splits with one leg up on a mat to make her split more than 180 degrees.

Kim was asked how the balance beam mistake would affect her other routines. "That was only one event and the rest are completely different and completely different scores," she replied. "And I think if I do strong enough routines on the other ones I can still make it through."

Although Kim's confidence may have been shaken on beam, her floor routine was as strong as ever. A good performance on floor was just what she needed to get back into the competition.

Bela gave her a quick hug and did not allow her time to revel in her performance. "Let's go," he said, referring to the next event, the vault. On the way to the vault, Bela gave Kim some words of encouragement about her floor routine: "That was a nice one. Good." Kim scored a 9.925.

Shannon completed another fine routine, this time on balance beam, then an equally strong performance on floor. She was quietly picking up the slack and leading the United States team in the process.

Kim's bothersome injuries were evident as she stood at the foot of the vaulting runway, awaiting her turn. She wore two bulky wrist guards, and her left ankle was taped up to her calf muscle.

When the green light came on, Kim sped down the runway and punched the board hard to propel herself high off the three-foot nine-inch vault. She did a Yamashita with a half twist and looked for the landing. Unfortunately, her sore left foot could not withstand the pressure, and she had to shuffle a bit on the landing. Still, Kim cleared the two-meter distance marker and received a 9.90.

On vault, the gymnasts must land a certain distance from the horse or they receive a deduction. Also, in the compulsories, the women, similar to the men, only get one chance to vault. In the optionals, women have two opportunities.

Shannon stuck her vault for a 9.95.

Kim rotated to her final event, the uneven bars. She chalked her hands one last time, glanced over to Bela for some reassurance, then raised her arms to begin. Her routine was solid, although she did not reach a complete handstand on a couple of moves. But her full-twisting flyaway dismount was excellent. The judges liked the performance and gave her a 9.887.

Kim and Bela were quite solemn as he helped her put on her warm-up jacket. Their silence and grim faces spoke volumes about her earlier beam performance.

After the meet, Kim spoke quietly about the fall. "I just went a little too quickly into the movement," she said, "and it made me go a little crooked."[11]

Bela was not happy. "The beam was the one I was concerned about," he said. "Sometimes, it leaves sour memories, and kicks back the next day."

Kim could not remember the last time she had fallen off beam in a competition. "That," she said with a small but defiant voice, "is not something we try to remember."[12]

When asked if she had experienced problems in practice with the beam sequence that caused her to fall, Kim said, "No, that's the thing. I don't even remember—of course, I had fallen on it before—but I don't remember, because with compulsories you don't think about making the routine. You're thinking about every little detail; how to make this bigger or how to make sure that your toes are extended. You don't think about just staying on the apparatus. So when I fell I really didn't remember the rest of the routine too well because I was almost in a daze."[13]

After the first day of competition, the United States was in second place, five tenths behind the Unified team. Romania was breathing on the neck of the United States, with less than one tenth separating the two teams. Not surprisingly after her strong performances, Shannon was in first place. Kim was a distant thirty-second. Although far from first place, the attention of the press still seemed drawn to Kim and her problems.

The Olympic Games mark the last time a set of compulsories is performed. Afterwards, new compulsory routines to be used for the next four years are developed for each event. In order to be fair, a different country is selected to compose the routines for each of the four apparatuses.

Kim was not at all sad to be finished with these particular routines. "I'm not going to have to do those compulsories ever again," she stated. "I couldn't see dwelling on that stuff."

A day separated the compulsories from the optional round of the team competition. Kim and Bela went into the gym on this "day off" to work hard to restore her confidence and prepare for the battle in the team optionals. A strong performance there would secure her place in the all-around final. Kim, wearing a yellow tank body suit, concentrated especially hard on balance beam, going through several routines to ensure that she would not make any more mistakes.

In the team finals, Kim would need to place in the top three on the American squad in order to qualify to the all-around competition. To do this, Kim would have to bump off Kerri Strug, who was in the third spot, but at the same time join forces with Kerri to battle the Unified and Romanian teams. Shannon Miller and Betty Okino had the first and second spot, respectively.

Kim and Kerri both trained at the same gym under Bela. Kim said it would be difficult "knowing only three from every country can go. We're all teammates, but we're all fighting for the same thing."[14]

There had been some tension between these two athletes because of a statement Kerri had made about Kim during the 1992 Individual Apparatus World Championships in Paris. Describing the difference between Kim and herself, Kerri had said, "Sometimes in a meet I'll do better, but overall I'm more consistent in the workout, which is kind of annoying, because you know you can do it. And then Kim, who goes out there and shows something different than she does in workout—it's really aggravating. You say, 'Well, hey, I'm just as good as her. Why does she always win?'"[15]

Kim, of course, had not been happy with Kerri's comment. But Kerri had not intended for the statement to sound that way. She clarified her intent in an interview with *International Gymnast* magazine.

"It came out kinda different than I had hoped for, because I didn't really realize I had said it that way," Kerri had said apologetically. "I *do* sometimes get upset because Kim *always*, no matter what she does in workout—I mean, she trains hard and does well—but no matter what she does, she always can pull it out in a meet, and sometimes it's annoying. But . . . I really admire her for that . . . that's what it takes, I guess."[16]

Fortunately, Kim and Kerri had resolved their differences, and they were now ready to face the competition as teammates.

The United States began its quest for an Olympic team medal on uneven bars. Kim was wearing a new lucky hairpin that she hoped would help her into the all-around final.

Kerri performed an excellent uneven bar routine, but she stumbled a bit on the dismount for a 9.862. Kim answered with a clean set, but like the other Americans before her, she had to take a small hop on the dismount.

"It was very good, Kimbo," Bela said, but he told her to stay down on the landing. Kim smiled and nodded her head in agreement. Bela slapped her on the back as she left to prepare for the next event.

Kim completed her bar routine without any major errors. She breathed a sigh of relief as she took off her bar grips, which were used to protect her hands and helped her grasp the bar. To the sound of cameras clicking in the background, she began taping her wrist for balance beam. Her every move was being tracked by the media.

With a score of 9.90, the gap between Kim and Kerri decreased. Unfortunately, the Americans' lead over the Romanians was also decreasing; several Americans did not stick their landings.

Kim moved to the balance beam, the event that could possibly ruin her Olympic dream. She fell off during the touch warm-ups, which heightened the stress she already felt from the nagging memory of her disastrous compulsory beam routine from two days ago.

Kim tried to remain optimistic. "The warm-up is not the competition," she said. "I realize that."[17]

Kerri went before Kim and had a solid set, although she took a sizable hop on the dismount and received a 9.75.

Kim did not watch Kerri's routine. She kept going through her own routine on an imaginary beam on the sidelines and tried to concentrate on her upcoming performance. Kim followed Betty's calm and smooth routine, breezing past her best friend without even acknowledging her as she mounted the podium. Kim was deep in concentration, and Betty respected that.

"Rhythm of the back handspring and tight," Bela barked sternly to Kim as she waited for the judges to turn on the green light.

After they signaled her to start, Kim took a deep breath and bounced off the springboard to her opening pose. Kim flowed through her routine gracefully and confidently. Then she stuck her dismount cold.

Kim ran for Bela's arms, which proved to be difficult since he was behind a barrier. Only one head coach for each team was allowed on the floor, and since Shannon was after Kim, her coach was on the floor preparing Shannon for her routine.

"That's how it's supposed to be!" Bela exclaimed gleefully about Kim's performance. "I love it!" He lifted Kim over the barrier and unknowingly squeezed her too tight, causing her to grimace in pain.

Kim got a 9.912, and some fans whistled and booed because they thought it should have been higher. Kim had almost caught up with Kerri, but Kerri was a good sport and told Kim she had done a good job. Although this was the team competition, much attention was drawn to Kim's struggle to make the all-around final.

The Romanians were tumbling up a storm on floor while the United States was on beam. Since the U.S. gymnasts again had trouble sticking their dismounts and had an assortment of wobbles, they dropped to third behind Romania. The Unified team was still firmly in first place as it had been from the beginning.

The Americans moved to the floor. Kerri danced and tumbled conservatively for a 9.837. Kim was capable of taking the lead if she could capitalize on Kerri's low score. Kim also had the added advantage of being the World Champion on this event.

Kim followed a wonderful routine by Shannon Miller, but there was a delay before the judges lit the green light. Kim shook her legs, tipped her head from side to side, and jumped up and down to stay warm. Once she was ready to go, it was hard for her to stand on the podium with everyone watching and be at the mercy of the judges. But she had to wait until they were ready.

"Move a little bit, Kimbo," Bela called to her as she continued to wait.

Finally, the judges were set. Kim stepped on the floor and stood in the corner with her hands at her side and her chin up. The music played for a few seconds, and then she began to move. She elected to do easier tumbling than in the Olympic Trials because of the stress fracture in her leg. She seemed to be all business; she did not play to the crowd as much as usual.

Kim ended strongly and was welcomed by Bela, who said, "All right! That was a good one. Now be careful; vault is coming up, Kimbo." She rushed to gather her bag and march to the fourth and final event, the vault.

Kim had surpassed Kerri after floor exercise for the third spot on the United States team. All she had to do was maintain her lead, and she would qualify for the all-around final and be one step closer to making her Olympic dream come true.

Kerri, not willing to give up the fight, stuck her vault for a 9.95. Kim had her work cut out for her: she needed a 9.936 to beat Kerri.

"Lift, watch for the landing," Bela shouted to Kim after he set her springboard at the right marker.

Kim saluted the judges twice and rechecked her starting position. She executed a strong vault, but she had to slide her feet back a little.

Bela gave her some tips for her second attempt, and Kim walked slowly back to her beginning distance. She took a deep breath, tugged on her leotard to make sure it was in place, and put a little chalk on her hands to keep them from slipping. The score posted for her first vault was a 9.937, and again the audience booed.

Kim, oblivious that she had made the all-around final, ran hard on her second try, pushed her four-foot seven-inch frame as far away from the vault as she could, and nailed the landing. She even smiled at the judges.

Bela gave her a big hug. "You're gonna be there," he said, referring to the all-around competition. "You're gonna be there."

Martha put her arm around Kim and rubbed her back. Kim bit her lip trying to fight back the pain in her leg, but she still had to limp.

"Oh my God, I can't walk," Kim said after hugging her teammate Wendy Bruce. But then she turned and smiled for the camera as if nothing was wrong.[18]

Being a little stingy, the judges gave her only a 9.95. Still, Kim placed first ahead of the entire field in the optional round of the team competition.

Kim was the best in the world on this day, July 28, 1992.

If she could repeat this feat and win the optionals again in two days, she would be the next Olympic Champion.

Shannon Miller placed first overall when the compulsories and optionals were combined, proving the Americans were definitely a force with which to be reckoned.

"Both Kim and Shannon are going to fight for the [gold] medal position," Bela said. "The placement right now—Shannon won the compulsories; Kim won the optionals—shows the capabilities of these two young athletes."

Steve Nunno seemed satisfied with the outcome thus far and changed his earlier position, saying, "It's not a rivalry. It's a one-two punch. A dynamic duo."[19]

Kim was pleased to make the all-around final along with teammates Betty and Shannon. She seemed to be her cheery self again.

"It has been a tremendous effort," she said. "I've been training a lot. I put into practice what I usually do in training and I made it."

Bela added enthusiastically, "Kim had the chance to reach the individual finals, and we've had to make a really big effort. The results have been fantastic, especially tonight."[20]

Although Kim advanced to the next segment, she realized that someone had to be bumped in order for her to make it. Unfortunately, that someone was her friend and teammate, Kerri Strug.

"I feel bad for Kerri," Kim said. "I'd rather it didn't have to be anybody, but it did."

"For most of the night, it felt like me against Kim out there," Kerri responded. "I came to the Olympics wanting to make it to the all-around. I'm happy for the bronze medal, but it's very hard to take."[21]

In the team standings, the Unified team captured the gold for the tenth of the ten times they had entered the event.

Romania took the silver, and the United States won the bronze.

Kim was proud to stand on the podium and receive her first Olympic medal. She was the last one on the U.S. team to have the medal draped around her neck. The presenter congratulated her, and she nodded her head with a smile as if to say thank you. She hoped to win more medals over the next several days in Barcelona.

The last time the United States women's gymnastics team had won a medal in a non-boycotted Olympics had been in 1948 when it took home the bronze. The Soviets had not taken part in those Olympics, however.

In the 1988 Olympics in Seoul, South Korea, the United States had placed fourth in a controversial situation. The women's team had amassed enough points to win the bronze medal, but Ellen Berger, an East German official who at the time was president of the Fédération Internationale de Gymnastique (FIG) Women's Technical Committee, had noticed a technical violation. The alternate to the United States team, Rhonda Faehn, had pulled the springboard off the mat after Kelly Garrison had begun her uneven bar routine and had stayed up on the podium crouched behind the board to watch. Apparently, there was an obscure rule disallowing someone to remain on the podium during an athlete's routine. A jury had met after the compulsory competition and decided to take five tenths off the American team's score. Ironically, the German team had benefitted from this decision. They had been in the fourth spot, and the five-tenth penalty had been just enough for the Germans to surpass the Americans. Still, the members of the United States team had known in their hearts that they deserved the bronze.

Kim and her teammates had won the bronze medal but they were not satisfied. They had been aiming for gold or, at least, silver.

"The kids were a little bit down, and I told them there was no reason to be sorry,"[22] Bela said. His view of the team bronze medal was different from theirs: "That's a medal. That's what we've all been really dreaming about. The color of the medal this time does not matter. It was a great fight. The kids done extremely well; they humanly done everything that they could. And all just as I predicted—who knows where we are gonna finish, and the last event is gonna be the one which gonna decide it—exactly that's what happened. But I'm very, very happy. I'm very proud of the kids, and overall that is all probably one of the best we ever had."[23]

After the team final, Bela shockingly announced his retirement. "This medal, tonight's medal, is probably nicer than all the other ones because that's the end of my career," he said somberly. "It is a definite decision."

"I am fifty," he explained. "I have thirty years of coaching—I started out when I was twenty—without interruption, maybe six months, when I came to the United States. Also, I have six Olympic Games behind me, with the stress, the dedication, and all the efforts which are included in it. Probably in the last twenty years I had no one moment which was not dedicated to preparation. Gymnastics, gymnastics, gymnastics. No vacations, no traveling, no anything. It's not a burden on me and I consider it a privilege to be in gymnastics. I've been doing it because of my strong belief in competitive sport and the excitement it offers. Athletes and coaches alike, I enjoyed every moment of it . . . I have no intention to run away from the sport I love so much, but I'd like to do something that might be different . . . to dedicate my time and energies in a different way to the advancement of gymnastics."[24]

Kim was not shocked that Bela had decided to call it quits. "It wasn't a really, really big surprise, but it was a surprise—I don't know if that sounds right," she said. To clarify her statement, she added, "We knew it would come sometime, 'cause we had heard something already after the '88 [Olympics] that he was thinking one more Olympics. It's still kind of hard to hear it even when it did come out. I guess that was kind of hard on us a little bit 'cause we're thinking, 'Well, he's had so many successes and we're kind of the last one and we better make it good.' That was kind of hard."[25]

There was a day between the team competition and the all-around final. Kim, Shannon, and Betty spent Wednesday rehearsing their routines and fixing up any rough areas. In a bright blue leotard, with her injured ankle heavily taped, Kim went through numerous routines on all the events as Bela watched her every move. She blocked out the pain in her foot in order to correct the small mistakes one last time before the all-around competition the next day.

As she went to bed that evening, Kim had doubts about performing under enormous pressure in front of millions of people worldwide while trying to ignore the painful injuries that plagued her body. But she had no idea what was in store for her. She could not have known how important a white line drawn on the floor mat would be to the outcome of her dream.

150

Chapter 9

BATTLE FOR THE GOLD

A gold medal in the Olympic all-around final is the most prestigious and coveted prize in all of gymnastics. Typically, the all-around final is the most popular event during the Olympics. On Thursday, July 30, 1992, thirty-six of the world's most talented gymnasts gathered for this event at the Palau Sant Jordi in Barcelona, Spain. Most had trained and dedicated their lives for this competition.

Betty Okino, Shannon Miller, and Kim left the Olympic Village that afternoon aboard an Olympic van. Upon arriving at the Palau Sant Jordi, cameras surrounded the girls. Kim, wearing a Barcelona T-shirt and her Olympic credentials around her neck, jumped out of the van and grabbed her bag containing her leotard, grips, and other necessities for the evening. With her game face on, she focused straight ahead and walked toward the entrance. She managed to acknowledge the press, however, with a brief smile.

Kim had anxiously awaited this day. She was thankful to have a second chance to redeem herself after her break in compulsories. Her strong performance in the optional portion of the team competition had allowed her to squeak by teammate Kerri Strug and into the all-around final.

Like Kim, Tatiana Gutsu had fallen off the balance beam in the team competition. However, she had not placed in the top three on the Unified team and consequently had not made the all-around final. Nevertheless, the Unified team felt she was one of its brightest hopes for a medal, so Tatiana was substituted for Roza Galieva who supposedly hurt her knee.

For the first time in the Olympic Games, the New Life rule was implemented: all the gymnasts would start equally and the scores from the previous team competition would be erased. This meant that only one day of competition, the all-around final, would decide the champion. In the past, the gold medal had been awarded to the gymnast who performed the best throughout three grueling rounds: team compulsories, team optionals, and the all-around competition.

The new system benefitted Kim and Tatiana Gutsu since they had both fallen in the team competition. But many were opposed to the idea, since the Olympic Champion would now have to hit only four routines instead of twelve to win the title.

Kim kept her arms moving as she waited for the judges' signal to begin on floor, her first event of the evening. Her left ankle and left wrist were heavily taped to support the stress fractures in them. She was not going to let the injuries stop her, though. She had worked ten long years for this moment, this chance to win the gold medal. This might be her only attempt at Olympic glory, since the possibility of hanging on for four more years until the next Olympics was slim.

"Solid, Kimbo. Don't forget the dance part. Solid landings, tight stomach," Bela reminded her.

Kim nodded and tried to stay focused. She knew how crucial it was to have Bela by her side.

"It's really important for me to have Bela there," Kim had once said. "Right before I go, I look at him one last time, and that usually gives me that extra confidence that I can do it."[1]

After what seemed like an eternity, Kim was allowed to begin. She stood firm and attentive as her music began, then she opened with a high full-twisting double pike somersault. Once again, she took out her upgraded tumbling of a whip to a double layout because of her leg injury, but she danced happily and electrified the crowd with her three whip backs to a double back. All she had left was her final tumbling pass, a simple double back.

Then a costly error occurred. On her final landing, Kim's foot accidentally crossed over the white boundary.

She was used to ending with a demanding full-twisting double and consequently had too much height, causing her to bounce out of bounds. Kim knew the penalty could cost her the gold. When the routine was finished, she walked off the floor despondently.

Bela gave Kim a brief hug that lacked his normal excitement. Not knowing what to say, he joked that the full-twisting double back would have been better at the end.

"All right, now vaulting," Bela said, attempting to hide his extreme disappointment.

"I'm last," Kim responded in regard to her placement on the next event.

"You are very last. Okay, then I've got to go to the bars, so don't worry about it. I'm going to come back," Bela told Kim. He needed to help Betty get ready for her next apparatus.

"She's on the floor," Kim corrected.

"Oh, she's on the floor, then I'm going to go with her then, okay?" Bela asked, patting Kim on the back as he turned to walk away.

The cameramen, not wanting to miss a beat or give Kim any space, surrounded her. She tried to pretend they were not there, but she could not conceal her worried expression. She sat down to rest and stared into space with a blank look on her face. Kim glanced unenthusiastically at the 9.775 that was posted, which put her in twenty-third place.[2]

Kim admitted after the team competition that she had never felt so much pressure in her whole life as in this meet. "The floor deduction was only a tenth of a point, but even if I didn't go out [of bounds], my score still wouldn't have been very high,"[3] she said.

Svetlana also began on floor exercise and turned in an average performance that lacked difficulty in the tumbling. She received a 9.912.

With Kim out of the hunt, the media refocused on two blondes from different parts of the globe who looked so similar they could pass as sisters: Shannon Miller and Tatiana Gutsu. They both began on uneven bars with near-perfect routines that were packed with hard tricks. The media had not been paying as much attention to these two because they were both soft-spoken and very similar. They did not provide as sharp a contrast as did the long-legged, graceful Svetlana Boginskaya and the stocky, powerful Kim Zmeskal.

In the second round, Tatiana corrected her problems on balance beam from the team competition, this time earning a 9.912. Shannon had some wobbles but still scored a 9.925. Svetlana stuck her vault for a 9.962 and the lead.

Meanwhile, Kim sprinted down the vault runway, flew through the air, and firmly stuck her eighty-pound frame to the mat for a 9.937. With the strong vault, she was able to move up into eighth position.

Svetlana played it cautiously with only one release move

on her third event, uneven bars, but she was flawless. The judges gave her a 9.887, and Svetlana was not happy.

Kim also competed on uneven bars. She rose to the occasion and performed one of the best routines of her life. She had two high release moves and a stuck double pike dismount. She smiled as she saluted the judges. They gave her a 9.90.

Shannon, who was quickly and quietly moving up in the standings, completed a delightful floor routine to keep her medal possibilities alive.

Although Kim had performed valiantly on the vault and bars, her floor mistake was too costly to overcome. She mounted the balance beam, her final apparatus of the night, with no chance of winning a medal. Even a perfect 10 would not clinch the bronze medal, let alone the gold.

Kim began strong, but the disappointment was too great for her to stand. She only threw one of her back layouts and omitted the second one. Her lack of concentration continued, and she wobbled on her back handspring whip and hopped on the dismount.

Kim walked toward Martha and Bela with her head hung down and her eyes glued to the floor.

Bela shook her gently and said what she already knew: "Kimbo, Kimbo, that wasn't a good one." He hugged her anyway and urged, "Okay, head up."

Kim caught a glimpse of the 9.80 on the scoreboard and then reached down to grab her belongings. She did not shed a tear; she was tough, but the tremendous disappointment and sadness she felt were reflected in her big, round eyes.

Kim finished tenth. Interestingly, the best American finisher in the 1988 Olympics had been Brandy Johnson, who had also placed tenth. America's best hope that year, Phoebe Mills, had fallen on balance beam, ruining her medal chances.

Svetlana started out well on her final event, balance beam, but she had a bobble on a leap that knocked her out of the top standings. After her routine, before the score was posted, Kim walked over to Svetlana to congratulate her. She kissed Svetlana on both cheeks, and Svetlana thanked her. Svetlana received a 9.912 and ended up fifth.

The overly-hyped duel between these two athletes had not been expected to end this way. But Kim thought the press had been trying to force a battle between the two of them that was not really there.

"That's one thing that's kind of bothered me for a long time is that people think that we don't get along," Kim revealed long after the meet was over. "It's really friendly between us. Of course, we can't communicate very well because of the language barrier, but I really respect her as a person and as an athlete, and I think it's the same way from her aspect. I wish people would realize that a lot of it was from the media, I think, wanting to create some big story about the rivalry, or whatever. Of course it was there in the competition; everyone wants to be the best."[4]

The crowd in Barcelona and around the world tuning in by television was anxiously awaiting the crowning of the Olympic Champion. The past three Olympics had come down to the same final event, the vault: Mary Lou Retton versus Ecaterina Szabo in 1984, Elena Shushunova versus Daniela Silivas in 1988, and now Tatiana Gutsu versus Shannon Miller.

Shannon went first. Under enormous pressure, she ran down the runway and did one of the best vaults of her career for a 9.975. Her second vault was not quite as good. She scored a 9.95, so the first score was counted. All she could do now was wait and watch her opponent.

Tatiana mounted the podium needing a 9.939 to move ahead of Shannon. She performed a high vault, the same one as Shannon, but a tiny hop kept her at a 9.925. On her second and final attempt, Tatiana stuck her vault cold for a 9.95 and the prestigious gold medal.

Shannon, however, had the highest point total when the scores from all three days were combined, proving she was one of the best in the world. Tatiana only outscored Shannon on the third day, the day that counted.

A former East German Olympian, Steffi Kraeker, stated it best about the New Life rule: "[The female gymnasts] used to have to perform twelve perfect routines to become the World Champion, and now a gymnast can have mistakes and still become World Champion."[5]

Shannon would have won under the old system. Interestingly, under the New Life rule, Ecaterina Szabo would have beaten Mary Lou Retton in 1984, and Daniela Silivas would have defeated Elena Shushunova in 1988, not the other way around.

Kim proved she could be as good a loser as she was a winner. In the spirit of good sportsmanship, she said, "I'm really glad that Shannon has gotten the attention she's gotten, because she really deserves it, and she's a really terrific athlete. You know, it's funny that people always think that she just popped out of nowhere . . . she was always there with the skills and everything, and I'm glad that she's gotten all the respect that she has right now."[6]

Kim was not thrilled with her own performance. "I made a couple mistakes," she admitted, "but all together the scores weren't going very high even when I did do my best."[7]

Tatiana Gutsu shared why she thought Kim's scores were lower. "I think her gymnastics is at a lower level," she said. "Maybe I'm wrong."[8]

Kim looked on the bright side: "I did try my best, and that's all that counts."[9] She proved that she could be graceful even in defeat.

Bela did not like the outcome of the meet. "I am definitely going to retire from gymnastics, particularly after the frustration I felt in seeing a gymnast as good as Kim Zmeskal lose,"[10] he complained.

The media and many of Kim's fans had considered her the easy favorite in Barcelona, because she had won the World Championships in the all-around and in both balance beam and floor exercise.

"I think a lot of people forget that with a sport like gymnastics that the scores are so close," Kim reminded everyone. "But luckily, at least, gymnastics does get publicity, especially during the Olympic year. And, if anything, I'm glad that at least what we did in Indianapolis was able to give us more support going into the Olympics. But, of course, with that comes the pressure of living up to expectations."[11]

There was a rumored accusation after the Olympics that Bela had left the competition when Kim had not won the all-around final, thus stranding her in her greatest time of need.

Bela was offended by the allegation. "I believe it is very inaccurate," he later responded to the charge, "and it's an [insult] even to bring up something to run away from the kids at the time of having difficulties. That's probably the [most painful] thing I've heard for a long, long time. Of course, I wasn't the most popular coach at the time . . . but I never did hear something like that. It would be interesting to ask not the ones who've been around and guessing this type of situation just like you described. It would be nice to ask the athlete herself who [has] been in it."

Bela was also chastised after the Olympics for not giving big bear hugs for a poor performance, but he felt he had to reward the great performances by setting them apart. He would put his arm around the athlete to console her and give corrections after a less-than-par performance, but his mood was naturally not exuberant after a serious mistake had been made.

"Sure, the time when she [Kim] fell [on compulsory beam], it wasn't anything to get excited, to jump up and down," Bela explained. "It was a deep meditation. Why this situation did happen? And I did know the reasons [why] this happened. The pressure . . . the controversial ups and downs between hot and cold, the unfair stage where she had already been placed before the competition started, the other very low stage where actually the judging community . . . destroyed her confidence to a certain extent [by not giving her good scores]."[12]

* * *

The event finals, the fourth and final component of the Olympic competition, were on Saturday, August 1. By this time, fatigue was a factor. The stress and pressure had taken its toll, and the athletes were ready to sight-see in Barcelona and then go home.

Up to this point, the United States women's gymnastics team had always been under strict supervision. They had not visited tourist attractions or socialized much because they were in Barcelona for a job that needed to be done. There would be time after the competition to view historic sights and see more of the Olympic Village.

The women's gymnastics team was the talk of the town and was being criticized by other American sports teams for being too serious. The swimmers said that on the airplane to Barcelona, the gymnasts had just sat there and not enjoyed themselves. And at the cafeteria, Bela's gymnasts had supposedly stared down at their plates and had not talked or laughed.

"It is supposed to be fun at the end when the competition is over and enjoy the result and enjoy all that you've been working around," Bela responded. "Competition is still competition. You're talking about the Olympic Games. It is not a flea market joint exhibition. It's a tough competition with the best athletes in the world. It is a serious, demanding, focusing type of activity. You cannot fool around in order to be ready for it."[13]

Bela remarked, "The 1992 Olympic Village in Barcelona, Spain, was pervaded by jealousy and suspicion. In the past, all athletes competing in the Games lived in the Village. They adhered to strict rules—no drinking, no late-night parties, no male/female fraternizing. In 1992 the rules changed. Professional athletes took rooms in the most exclusive hotels in Spain, while amateur athletes stayed in the Village's dorms. For the first time, living in those dorms did not feel like the honor it was. Then there were the parties. Every night I had to ask athletes in the dorm to be quiet so my gymnasts could sleep. There was no respect for fellow athletes or for the Games."[14]

The top eight finishers in the team competition on each event qualified to the event finals. Since Kim had fallen off the balance beam during the team compulsories, she did not make the beam finals. She qualified on vault and floor exercise, however.

Kim had the advantage of going last on vault. She did a nice full-twisting layout Yurchenko with only a small hop to the side. The judges gave her a 9.925. Her second vault was a handspring front somersault that was only valued at a 9.90. Unfortunately, Kim bent her knees right off the board and did not get much height. She landed on her seat, which counted as a fall.

Kim had not practiced her second vault much because she only had to perform it in event finals, which are not held very often. Bela smiled and rolled his eyes when he saw her fall. Kim's mom also shook her head in frustration. Kim finished last on the vault and was the only one to fall down.

Bela massaged Kim's sore leg as she waited for her turn on floor exercise, the other event to which she qualified. Kim would be last on this event as well. She used more difficult tumbling by opening with a whip back to a full-twisting double back, but she did not use the double layout that she had shown at the Olympic Trials, which was more difficult. Kim ended with a full-twisting double pike and almost stepped out of bounds. She did not seem as enthusiastic as usual.

Neither did Bela. He gave Kim a quick hug but was not very pleased. She was awarded a 9.90 for sixth place.[15]

Bela sat down wearing a defeated expression on his face as he waited for the awards ceremony. What a strange sight it was to see Bela so depressed at an Olympics. This giant in the sport of gymnastics, this creator of World and Olympic Champions, had the look of someone who had lost all hope. It did not seem right to have worked so hard for so many, many years only to see the hopes and dreams fade away, especially now, at the end. What was to have been the climax of a legendary career was instead a hollow disappointment.

But Bela had chosen to retire; he could just as easily choose to come out of retirement. And with the United States hosting the next Olympics in 1996, there was the slightest possibility that he would do just that.

It had been a tough week for Kim, but she managed to keep her chin up. "I'm happy the team won a bronze and I'm happy and proud for Shannon,"[16] Kim said, trying to be positive. She signed a few autographs and quietly exited the arena.

Kim was calm and professional throughout the Olympics and during the interviews. When asked if she ever broke down at all, she smiled and said, "Oh yes,"[17] revealing that she was human after all.

Although Kim had been suffering from a stress fracture in her left leg throughout the Olympics, she refused to let that be an excuse for her performance.

"She bravely and silently was competing despite a nasty ankle injury,"[18] Bela stated.

The injury was the biggest disappointment to Kim. "That was probably one of the most frustrating parts," she said, "because I was really looking forward to being able to compete the routine that I did at Trials. That's what I had been looking forward to doing since 1990, being able to put that tumbling in my routine [whip through to double layout mount, pike full-twisting double back dismount]. And it was going very well . . . it was fun for me to do and it wasn't that hard. And then to go over there and be injured, of course, I didn't get to train as much as I would have liked to. I don't want to blame it on the injury because a lot of things were involved, but that's one of the hardest parts because injuries—there's not a whole lot you can do about. I mean, you can work through it, but there's just a certain point where your body won't let you do it."[19]

Part of the excitement of being in the Games was staying in the Olympic Village, meeting other athletes from different countries, and discovering the culture of Spain. Kim and her teammates also got a chance to meet several celebrities.

"We heard the whole [dream] team was at accreditation and we went over and saw a bus sitting there," Kim said about the experience. "We waved and they sort of waved back and we saw Larry Bird waving . . . I think he recognized me and Betty. We walked over there and Michael Jordan said, 'Hi, I'm Michael,' like we didn't know. It was really fun."[20] Kim also saw other famous people like Magic Johnson, Carl Lewis, Arnold Schwarzenegger, Christian Slater, Tom Cruise, and Nicole Kidman.

Like Bela, Kim had said she might retire after the 1992

Olympics. Although the next Olympics would be in Atlanta, that was not enough incentive to continue training until the age of twenty. Her social life and family time had been sacrificed for the sport, and now she wanted to experience more of both.

Although Kim did not do as well as expected at the Olympic Games, she received a warm welcome at the Houston airport. Many of her fans who considered her a hero showed up to support her. Kim, with a new hairstyle—all her bangs pulled back in a clip—was all smiles and happy to be home. She seemed surprised to see so many people waving banners, flashing pictures, and trying to get a glimpse of Houston's littlest celebrity.

Kim summed up her Olympic performance by saying, "My whole life was not just for the Olympics, but it really, of course, was a very big deal to me. And, of course, with the expectations from everyone else I had expectations of myself, also, and I was planning on making it my last big competition, the best one. And with all the confidence I had from everybody else it seemed like it was all going to go very well. And of course, I was disappointed with how it ended up, but I'm still able to go on with my life and am grateful for all the other success I had."[21]

Although Kim had not fulfilled the media's expectations, little girls all over the country, and perhaps even the world, looked up to her and hoped to be just like her one day. She received much fan mail and support, and many new little gymnasts signed up to take gymnastics classes following the Olympics in order to become the next Kim Zmeskal.

What would Kim do following the Games? She had held on to one big superstition during the course of her gymnastics career: she would not allow trophy cabinets in her home until her competitive career was finished.[22] Maybe now it was time to bring in the trophies. Her mentor had retired. Would she?

Chapter 10

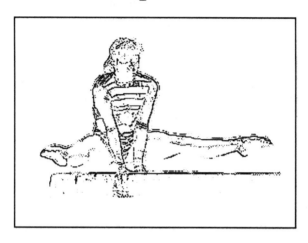

A COMEBACK

Even though Shannon Miller had won the most Olympic medals of any U.S. woman, Kim found herself on the cover of *Newsweek* magazine August 10, 1992 following the Games. She was pictured wearing a look of deep concentration and wiping chalk off her mouth with an uneven bar grip on her hand. The words "It Hurts—Do We Push Teen Athletes Too Hard?" were plastered across the page.

The press seemed drawn to Kim like a magnet. Maybe Shannon was too shy, while Kim's spunky personality seemed a more fitting image of the next great American gymnast, the one that could replace bubbly Mary Lou.

The *Newsweek* article bluntly stated that young bodies were not meant to endure the stress to the joints inflicted by the intense training of elite-level gymnastics. It also claimed that some parents were obsessed with their child being successful, and focusing on maintaining a low weight and low body fat was unhealthy and could lead to eating disorders.[1]

Kim did not like the article. "I didn't think that was fair," she remarked, "because I don't think a lot of people realize that it's not the only purpose that I'm alive . . . to be in the Olympics, and to win the Olympics. I'm still very happy, and nobody forced me to do it. They had said something in the article about child abuse, or people forcing us to do it. It's *never* been like that for me, and none of my teammates either. It's hard to get very good in something that you don't want to do, and so most of the time those girls end up dropping out anyway. Of course, you do see it sometimes in the gym where you think it's the parent who wants it more than the child, but they don't end up succeeding and you can tell because they're not happy. Gymnastics has always been something that *I* wanted to do. I was the one who asked my parents to let me start in the beginning, and I'm still the one who drives myself up there."[2]

Kim also said, "I think that we got a lot of abuse [from the press] that we're young and that we're female, but we all do it because we love it."[3]

Kim enjoyed her popularity following the Olympics. She appeared on the *Maury Povich* talk show with Trent Dimas, who had won a gold medal at the Games on high bar—the only medal for the men's gymnastics team.

During the Olympics, Kim had hinted that she would retire from amateur gymnastics following the Games. But she never made a formal announcement about retiring like Bela had done. She put off the decision, at least for awhile, which made her fans wonder what she would really do.

"With retiring," Kim said, "I had always thought that I wouldn't want to do gymnastics afterward, and so that was never one of my choices to stay with it after 1992, 'cause I always thought I was missing all these great things in high school and everything."[4]

Although Kim was not sure if she wanted to compete, she still wanted to be involved with the sport. She relaxed and took it easy, traveling with gymnastics exhibitions and tours. This break from competition allowed her to enjoy the sport without the pressure to win.

In the fall, Kim participated in the 1992 McDonald's Gymnastics Spectacular Tour. She decided to use her old floor music of *"In the Mood"* for exhibitions. She was still suffering from a stress fracture in her left leg, so she did easy tumbling, opening with three whip backs to a single back somersault. The crowd loved it anyway. She did a tag team routine, allowing Scott Keswick to perform her second and third tumbling passes so she could rest her sore leg.

Kim electrified the audiences at various sites during the Tour. Although her performance at the Olympics had not been spectacular, she was one of the favorites on the Tour and a main attraction at the exhibitions. Little girls now looked up to her as her generation had looked up to Mary Lou.

The Unified team appeared at a few of the stops along the way, and Kim had one memorable encounter with Svetlana Boginskaya.

"She asked me if I was gonna compete [in 1993]," Kim recalled, "and I said, 'Well, I'm not really sure what I want to do.' And she said, 'Please compete.' And that just kind of stood out in my mind."

Unfortunately, Kim did not complete the whole Tour because of the leg injury she had suffered in France while training for the Olympics.

Although Kim enjoyed being involved with gymnastics exhibitions, her competitive spirit remained restless. In the back of her mind she was debating whether or not to defend her World title in Birmingham, England, the site of the 1993

World Championships.

But Kim also had to think about her future after gymnastics. "I do plan to attend college," she said. "However, NCAA rules prohibit me from competing in gymnastics." She had accepted prize money during the American Cup competition, thereby forfeiting her collegiate eligibility.

As for long-term career plans, Kim expressed an interest in broadcasting. She also got a taste of being a coach when she instructed a few clinics.

"I enjoyed working with the young gymnasts,"[5] Kim said about the experience.

Kim cut her training back from eight hours a day to two hours. She wanted to be a normal teenager, but she still needed to stay in shape for exhibitions.

Kim told *Sports Illustrated* what it was like at first with all the spare time: "After two weeks it was already boring. I used to dream of the day when I could just flop on the living room couch after school and watch television from 5:00 to 9:00 p.m. But now that I can do it, I'm not interested."[6]

When asked by *International Gymnast* editor Dwight Normile what was the biggest adjustment she had to make, Kim said, "Well, like knowing what to do. Because for so long I never had to worry about anything because I knew that I was gonna get up in the morning, go to the gym. Then I'd go to a private [lesson] for a couple of hours, and I'd go to the gym in the evening, and then I rarely had a whole lot of homework because I only had three classes.

"It was really difficult at first going back to public school where I had a full course load again and kind of knowing what to do with myself. I didn't think I'd want to go to the gym at all. I was thinking, 'Well after the Olympics, forget it. I probably won't have anything to do with it.' But after a month of not going to the gym I was like, 'Gosh, I kind of miss it.'

So I was working out again."[7]

Kim's popularity was still soaring high many months after the Olympics. *Sports Illustrated for Kids* did a poll asking children whom they would most like to be for a day. Kim was the only nonprofessional athlete and the only female chosen in the top ten. She was ranked the eighth favorite; Michael Jordan was number one.[8]

As 1992 came to an end, Kim enjoyed a quiet holiday season with her family. It was nice not to have a rigorous training schedule to work around. She decided to spend some time with her best friend, Betty Okino, after Christmas. Kim did not get to see Betty much now that she lived at home with her family in Elmhurst, Illinois.

With the start of a new year, Kim decided not to defend her World title. Instead, she was one of the four women invited to participate in the 1993 Subaru World Open held March 27 in Minneapolis, Minnesota. This would be Kim's first professional competition, with $15,000 at stake for first place in the all-around.

The women competed in three events: uneven bars, balance beam, and floor exercise. The athletes were allowed to wear different costumes for each event, and they could mount and dismount the equipment as many times as they liked. Music was used on all events, and beam and floor routines were lengthened to two minutes each. Kim had stiff competition, including 1992 Olympic Champion Tatiana Gutsu, Henrietta Onodi of Hungary, and Betty Okino.

Kim started on bars, executing a nice Tkatchev and double pike flyaway. Then, showing some creativity, she did a back handspring to a back extension roll under the low bar and mounted the apparatus a second time. The judges liked her originality and gave her a 9.70 and the early lead over Henrietta Onodi.

A Comeback

On the next event, the balance beam, Kim chose to perform to *"One"* from *"A Chorus Line."* She did her trademark reverse planche and hit her two layouts in a row and a gainer layout. She made her roundoff double tuck somersault dismount look easy. Kim received a 9.70, second only to Betty's 9.75. Still, Kim had a good lead over Betty in the all-around standings.

The final event was floor exercise, Kim's favorite. Decked out in a poodle skirt and a pretty jeweled leotard, Kim leaped, danced, and tumbled to a medley of the music from her two most famous routines, *"Rock Around the Clock"* and *"In the Mood."* She began with a double pike somersault, and she whirled off her skirt just before her popular three whip backs to a double back. Then came another double back for her third pass. Kim displayed stamina by adding a fourth pass, a pretty layout step-out. The audience members at the Target Center leaped to their feet in recognition of her fine effort. The judges awarded her the highest score of the evening, a 9.90.

Kim won the all-around with 29.20 points out of a possible 30.0 and edged out Betty Okino for the gold. Tatiana Gutsu finished a distant third.

Besides the $15,000 in prize money, Kim also took home a pair of diamond earrings worth $3,000. She dominated the competition with the highest score on uneven bars and floor exercise and the second highest score on balance beam.[9]

After the Subaru World Open, Kim went on the Gold Gymnastics Tour from April through June. She did routines on balance beam and floor exercise. Her beam routine contained her trademark mount to a reverse planche, a back handspring layout, and a gainer layout. On floor she used the same music medley as she had in the Subaru World Open. Her injuries persisted even a year after Barcelona, however. Her leg was heavily taped for most of the exhibitions. She managed to pull around a nice double back to start her routine on floor, and she

169

performed her famous middle pass consisting of three whips, but this time only to a single back flip.

Joining Kim on the Tour were Bela and Martha, Nadia Comaneci, Bart Conner, Betty Okino, Hilary Grivich, and Bela's newest sensations: Dominique Moceanu and Jennie Thompson. These two up-and-comers had styles very similar Kim's.

Kim shared her opinion of performing in exhibitions: "I really enjoy them because I like performing, but it's not the same because in an exhibition it's kind of like it's great if you make it, 'Oh well' if you don't. In competition it's not that relaxed."[10]

Kim said during the Tour that she could not imagine life without gymnastics. People wondered if this meant she was thinking about returning to competition.

Bela was asked if Kim was going to retire for sure, but his answer was vague in regards to amateur competition. "She is still actively participating in many gymnastics events," he replied, "among those the Gold Gymnastics Tour, World Open Gymnastics Championships, etc., clearly stating she is still a very important part of the U.S. gymnastics program, promoting the sport and keeping its international prestige. No, she is not retired."[11]

But Bela was definitely retired. With sour memories of 1992 and the Olympic Games in Barcelona, he had taken time off and stayed away from the gym for awhile.

"In '92 the fire was not burning," Bela reflected. "And I could not ignite the fire. And I tried, I honestly tried. I could not ignite the fire. The fire was not there. I looked around and I did not find those challenging coaches, the ones [who] were fired up to be the best. The ones that came, 'Urrgh, tomorrow we're going to go out, we're going to fight!'" Bela punched the air with his fists for emphasis. "They were beggars. They were all begging for a job. All begging for any opportunity to take. All of them talking about leaving their own countries.

"Then I looked out on the kids." He crinkled his brow. "The conversations I heard going on about agents, about qualifications of the agents, the ability of the agents, managers. That was their primary interest. Not the possibility of becoming an Olympic Champion; it was always secondary concern. And I thought, 'What's going on? Is something wrong with me? Or the world changes?' And I think it's both."[12]

Bela was particularly critical of the gymnastics judges. "[Kim and Betty] went into the 1992 Olympics not as fighters who were planning to experience a great moment of their gymnastics lives, but to perform a swan song of their athletic careers . . . they made mistakes that I had never seen before; they had lost their concentration, their ambition, and their drive. They had been broken . . . [by] the lack of support of their own judges, and the mind games they had been forced to endure up until the Games."[13]

* * *

Kim continued her busy schedule during the summer. She flew to Los Angeles to be part of a new cable television show for children called XUXA.

"It is a very popular Brazilian show that is coming to the United States,"[14] Kim said.

She also participated in the first ever gymnastics fashion layout. Along with Bart, Nadia, Jennie Thompson, and Dominique Moceanu, she posed in apparel donated by leotard manufacturers for the *International Gymnast* Back-to-School Fashion Collection. The spread was very well received and appeared in two issues of the magazine.

Kim was not much taller than Jennie or Dominique, yet

they were much younger than she was. She remarked about her height, "I was three feet ten inches when I was nine years old. Since then I haven't managed to grow even one foot, but it doesn't bother me too much. I do feel short in large crowds and when I stand next to my best friend Betty Okino. Some of my classmates joke about my height, but they don't do it to insult me. As long as you keep your chin up and have confidence in yourself, people won't look down on you."[15]

Next on Kim's agenda was the U.S. Olympic Festival held from July 29 to August 1 in San Antonio, Texas. She watched the event with Betty. Kim had first been noticed and gained attention after winning the Festival in 1989.

USA Gymnastics, formerly the United States Gymnastics Federation, sent Kim to Kansas City for the Christy Henrich Benefit Fund luncheon on August 12. Christy was a former National and World Championships team member who was suffering from anorexia and bulimia and whose weight had dropped into the fifties. Kim and Nadia spoke at the sold-out luncheon to support and encourage Christy. Although the benefit helped raise over $30,000, Christy could not overcome her eating disorder and died about a year later.

The luncheon started a weekend called "A Celebration of Healthy Sport" during which Kim and some local gymnasts performed in an exhibition at Worlds of Fun Amusement Park. An excited audience crammed into the theater to witness the event and bombarded Kim with autograph requests afterwards. On Saturday, she made media appearances, gave clinics, offered advice, and interacted with fans throughout the day.

During the last week in August 1993, Kim and Betty traveled to Salt Lake City, Utah, for another U.S. Championships. Kim was not going to defend her title and make it four in a row; this time she was going as a spectator. Kim and Betty found it difficult to sit in the stands while their former teammates from the 1992 Olympics—Kerri Strug, Shannon Miller, Dominique Dawes, and Michelle Campi—showed off their new skills.

"It's hard to watch the people from my generation who are still competing," Kim said. "We were like, 'Why did we come to see this?' It was just kind of hard to watch your teammates still doing it, because we're like, 'I still like this.'"[16]

Kim participated in the event by helping to pass out awards and congratulate the champions from the meet. Shannon Miller won the all-around.

In the fall of 1993, Kim began her senior year at a public high school. Away from the gym, she was like any other teenager. She enjoyed shopping in the mall, but trying to find shoes for her size five foot was quite a challenge. Kim thought the group Boyz II Men was cool, and giggled when her favorite band from junior high, New Kids on the Block, was mentioned.

"I like laughing and being with my friends,"[17] Kim shared. She was not a loud person, but she was not an introvert, either. She was more inclined to listen than talk.

Kim was Catholic and believed her faith in God had an important effect on her attitude and her gymnastics. "I think it's helped me a great deal and I think that everything that's happened to me I need to credit God for," she said. "I'm pretty religious. I really enjoyed being able to go to Northland [Christian School] because it was required to take Bible. And I kind of miss having that. But it's funny, 'cause now in English we're studying about Biblical allusions and so it's really fun to be able to talk about that kind of thing, because I really think that everything that's happened to me is because God wanted it for me. And hopefully I'll be able to help other people out, or possibly make them happy, as well."

Kim was still not certain where she was going with gymnastics. "Right now I am still training, mostly for exhibi-

173

tions," she said. "I'm finishing my senior year of high school in June and will be making more definite plans about my future then."[18]

On October 7-9, Kim participated in the opening of two state-of-the-art training facilities costing $12.8 million at the Olympic Training Center in Colorado Springs, Colorado. This was part of a program designed to make the Olympic Training Center the best multi-sport training facility in the world. Kim and other past Olympic celebrities dazzled the crowd with a great exhibition and made themselves available to sign autographs for their countless fans.

On October 22-23, Kim was involved in a preview of Paul Ziert's new tour that was to come out in 1994. It was a tribute to the fabulous fifties and sixties. Kim and the entire cast danced and flipped to the tune of *"Rock 'n' Roll Is Here to Stay."* The opening twenty minutes were dedicated to songs from the movie "Grease," and Kim performed to *"Hopelessly Devoted to You."* She demonstrated her competitive form by executing two layouts in a row, a gainer layout, and a roundoff double tuck somersault off the balance beam. On floor she had a high level of difficulty with a nice double layout, her patented three whip backs to a double back, and another double tuck. These routines would have been competitive on any world stage.

After such a busy schedule, Kim looked forward to the holiday break. For Thanksgiving in 1993, Kim's family—her fourteen-year-old sister, Melissa, her ten-year-old brother, Eric (both of whom were younger and taller than Kim), and her parents—went to her grandmother's house to have Thanksgiving dinner.

"I love turkey, and my grandma is German and makes tons of Kolacky's," Kim said. "My grandma's house is in the country and all my cousins are there; it's really fun."

Since Kim was not active in amateur competition, she was able to spend more time with her family over the holiday season.

"For Christmas my family and I go to church on Christmas Eve and are allowed to open one present after church," Kim shared. "We also make cookies and write a letter to Santa on Christmas Eve. In the morning we open all of our Santa gifts."[19]

Kim tried to keep in touch with her friends from the gym, even after they left Houston. "My closest friends throughout my career have been Betty Okino, Erica Stokes, Amy Scherr, Hilary Grivich, Kelly Pitzen, and Kerri Strug," she said. "We still try to stay in touch as much as possible. My friendship with these girls will always be special to me because of all that we've been through together."[20]

After the holidays, Kim again spent some time with Betty, who lived in the Chicago area.

"We did this last year, too," Kim said, "and it was so much fun."[21] Both Kim and Betty went skiing, something neither of them had ever done before. During their years as competitive gymnasts, a dangerous sport like skiing could have injured them and jeopardized their careers, which would have greatly displeased Bela.

Kim was voted the most missed gymnast in 1993 during the *International Gymnast* readers' response poll. Her fans were hoping to see her in the new year.

Kim was invited to the 1994 Reese's World Champions Cup in Baltimore, Maryland, held on January 23. Bela had said after Kim's victory in this professional competition in 1993 that she was planning to repeat her performance in 1994. But she did not get in enough training during the holidays, and at Bela's suggestion she turned down the invitation. Her decision was a disappointment to her many fans.

In February, Kim traveled to Norman, Oklahoma, to the Bart Conner Gymnastics Academy. She was a main attraction at the first Nadia Comaneci Invitational. Kim watched the meet and presented the winners with prizes in support of their good work. She liked Oklahoma so much that she decided to attend college at the University of Oklahoma in the fall of 1994.

Betty Okino said, "I am a senior in high school and plan to go to college in the fall. Kim Zmeskal and I would like to go to the same college and room together. We won't be doing gymnastics in college because we're ineligible to compete in the NCAA program."[22]

Kim was asked to answer questions in a *USA Gymnastics* magazine column called "Chalk Talk." Readers wrote to her with questions about problems they were having in gymnastics, or they asked her what it was like competing in the Olympics. Kim also agreed to serve as honorary captain of Club Gymnastics, a new program aimed at involving recreational gymnasts in USA Gymnastics. These young athletes received a subscription to *USA Gymnastics* magazine, a T-shirt, and other perks including discounts on various gymnastics merchandise.

Kim, Bela, and Betty were represented by the International Management Group of New York City. They made themselves available to give clinics and demonstrations and to attend special club events, like grand openings, when asked.

Only a year and a half after the Olympics, many things had changed in Kim's life. She was now a senior at Westfield High School. When she was not traveling with gymnastics shows, she was able to be more involved with school activities.

"I've gotten to really enjoy theater at my school,"[23] she remarked.

Kim attended a full day of school, then she took her daily pre-gym nap and drove her red '93 Ford Probe to the gym where she had spent much of her childhood and teenage life.

She worked out for about three hours every evening during the week. Kim no longer went in the morning because morning sessions were usually spent on compulsories, and she was only practicing to keep in shape for exhibition appearances.

"I train on weekday evenings for three to four hours and Saturday mornings," she explained. "I've always done gymnastics because I thought it was fun, so now it isn't really any different. I'm definitely still working out to stay in shape, too."[24]

Kim was placed in a workout group with Dominique Moceanu, Karolyi's new star, who was several years her junior.

"It's going good," Kim said of her less stressful workouts. "I'm having fun." She also had fewer injuries because of the shorter and less demanding practice schedule. "I think that has a lot to do with why I'm enjoying it so much. I don't have as much pain," Kim laughed.

Bela was asked by a young fan if he missed working with Kim. "I don't miss Kim Zmeskal," he said, "simply because I'm fortunate to still have her in the gym every day during her practice hours. But I fully understand your frustration in missing her exciting and spectacular way of performing in competitions. The good news is, she is still performing in many gymnastics-related events, and hopefully you will have an opportunity to see her again."[25]

Throughout his years of coaching, Bela had received his fair share of criticism both in Romania and the United States. He had been accused of everything from raging egotism to violation of the child labor laws and intimidation of judges. But he and Kim seemed to enjoy a good relationship.

When asked by Dwight Normile if she saw Bela as a "mean ogre," Kim replied, "I definitely don't see him like that. He's a very caring person and he's always wanted the best for his athletes. When he would talk about any of his athletes' accomplishments, it was never *we* did this, *we* did that. He always gave credit to the athlete, and I really respect that because he had so much to do with it and so much to do with so many people's happiness. We have a really good friendship, and I'm always going out to his ranch and seeing him there, doing things."[26]

Bela still had his enemies, though. Some speculated that Bela "abused" his kids and that they "expired rather than retired."[27] Usually the ones who had been successful under Bela praised him, and the ones who had not done so well spoke unfavorably of him. One of the latter was Chelle Stack. Chelle had been on the 1988 Olympic team but had failed to make the team in 1992. She had switched back and forth between Bela's gym and several others. According to Bela, she had often left without giving him any notice.

"I'm scared to death of him," Chelle said in an NBC television interview. "I regret that I had to go through what I went through. There's no reason for someone to have to go through—not so much physical pain, but there is mental pain. It's not describable."[28]

In an interview for *Newsweek*, Chelle also said, "I didn't realize how much hatred I had toward him."[29]

Mary Lou thought much differently of Bela. "He absolutely brought his Romanian system to America, thank goodness," she said. "He's changed American gymnastics around. His system, it works, it creates champions."[30]

Mary Lou summarized her opinion with a smirk: "You don't hear too much complaints from the winners."[31]

Yet a national coach who wanted to remain anonymous said, "You watch Bela on t.v. and then you watch him in the gym, you see a different man. It is not pretty and it's not right."

Another coach said, "He's used to a totalitarian system. It

shouldn't work in this country."

Bela defended himself. "Jealousy," he claimed. "I am challenging the system, challenging their sweet mediocrity they are protecting so aggressively." Bela scowled. "Holy cat! All I am saying is you must push hard. And you must have the highest standards."[32]

Bela asked rhetorically, "These critics of mine, who do you think they are? They are jealous coaches, non-producers. When they say, 'Oh that Bela,' it is because I have made their lives miserable. [These coaches] now have to work as hard as me, all day long. They can't come into a workout in a suit and tie and say 'Ok, girls, try very hard now and do fifteen minutes of conditioning while I leave early to play some golf.' Those coaches, my friend, are finished."[33]

The former coach of Bart Conner from the University of Oklahoma and longtime friend of Bela's, Paul Ziert, thought of Bela as a Romanian cowboy. "But he is brilliant," Paul was quick to say. "And he represents absolute commitment to gymnastics."

Mike Jacki, the executive director of USA Gymnastics, recognized what Bela had accomplished. "The one thing over the past ten years that's had the most effect on U.S. gymnastics," he said, "overwhelmingly, is the presence of Bela Karolyi."[34]

The success Bela made of the United States women's gymnastics program in such a short time is phenomenal. From 1983-1992, Bela had seven of the ten United States Champions. Bela's kids won seven Olympic gold medals and fifteen World Championships. Without Bela Karolyi, the United States gymnastics program would not be where it is today, a respected system producing some of the world's top athletes.

* * *

In retrospect of her amateur career, Kim admitted that the World Championships were her most satisfying competition and the Olympics were her most disappointing "because of how many people are aware of what happened there, and I don't want to be remembered by my fall on compulsory beam, because it didn't mean as much to me. And it's just kind of hard when so many people remember that."

Kim clarified that the fall "was a very big deal to me, but I have so much support everywhere else and I still enjoy doing it [gymnastics]. It's not like it's torn me away from the sport and I hate it forever."

But the fall on compulsory beam still haunted Kim. "I do think about it a lot," she admitted. "I mean, in the whole picture I guess it didn't mean a whole lot, as for the all-around standings, but that seemed to start it all on a bad note."[35]

What did Bela think of Kim's career in gymnastics? "There was no doubt about it. [Kim] was one of the *most* consistent kids throughout the years I *ever* had,"[36] he said with conviction. "She was a very interesting performer. She never turned around halfway through a competition and declared victory or defeat. It didn't matter if she was leading by a landslide or on her backside. And if she was losing, she never accepted the situation. Kim would always try to turn a loss around; she would always continue to fight. The reality of a scoring situation never mattered to her."[37]

Bela offered this advice to rising stars in the gym: "Let them stay at their own clubs, appreciate the preparation they are getting in the smaller or larger community. Enjoy the gym environment. And those little kids can enjoy the status of the little queen of the team, the little star of the town."[38]

Kim said her advice to young gymnasts was "pretty much what Mary Lou told me: you need to keep a good attitude in the gym. You need to set reasonable goals that you'd like to achieve, and keep them in mind every day at practice."[39]

* * *

What will become of Kim Zmeskal? After the Olympics, Kim continued to maintain a high level of difficulty in her exhibition routines. They would have been competitive with any of the top gymnasts in the world.

When asked if she would return to competition, Kim replied, "It's not out of the question . . . I still get to perform [in shows] and I enjoy that, but it's not the same as competition. Once you get the competitive blood in you, it's always there. I really don't know what will come with my future, but either way I'm really enjoying gymnastics right now."

In order to compete in 1996 in Atlanta, Kim knew she would need to learn the new compulsory routines. "I'm in [the gym] all the time so I'm playing with them," she said.

In the spring of 1994, Bela and Kim both began to question their decisions to retire.

"I still feel like I'm too young to retire," Bela had once said with a smile and a twinkle in his eye. "And I still have something from the fire which was burning for [such] a long time. And now when I'm not in a competitive arena, I still feel like the challenge is still there. But I want to start something from brand-new, from the scratch and build as I believe gymnastics is going to go from now on. Little kids, the ones who are not doing gymnastics for money and fortune. The ones who are going to do gymnastics again for the fame and the glory of gymnastics. Maybe they will not be ready for '96, but sure they're gonna be around for the year 2000, which is gonna be another memorable Olympic Games. But guys, don't relax, I'll be back."[40]

Kim, along with many others, hoped Bela would reconsider

his retirement. "I think it would be good if he did [return to coaching]," Kim stated. "I think he's done a lot for gymnastics, and especially American gymnastics. And I think that we could still use him."[41]

Bela had kept busy since his retirement from elite-level gymnastics. "I am directing all of my efforts to run and direct my gymnastics summer camps," he said, "providing for the participating students a high quality coaching and an unforgettable, exciting experience. But if the need should arise prior to the 1996 Olympic Games, I will not hesitate to lend a helping hand to my former or current competitive athletes."[42]

That need did arise. On May 25, 1994, at the halfway point between the 1992 and the 1996 Olympics, Bela announced on *Good Morning America* that he was not ready to call it quits. Kim had convinced him to give it one more try.

"I wasn't ready to do it, and to be honest, I wouldn't do it for nobody else in the world," Bela stated. "The sport has always been something that represents a special thing for her. And the more she got away from it the more she did realize how important the sport is for her."

After watching figure skater Katarina Witt in the 1994 Winter Olympics, an inspired Kim had decided she also wanted to compete in another Olympics. But she did not just want to participate.

"If I'm gonna do it, I'm a competitor and of course I'd like to challenge for a win," Kim said boldly. "But right now I'm not thinking that far ahead. I'm not in any big rush. I mainly just want to make sure that I'm in the best shape possible and I get the skills and the routines down."[43]

Ironically, Bela had just completed a book entitled <u>Feel No Fear: The Power, Passion, & Politics of a Life in Gymnastics</u> that detailed his career as a gymnastics coach. "[It] is such an interesting coincidence," he commented. "The book's supposed to be an ending of my career and describing my coaching life. And suddenly, and just unexpectedly for me, now I'm back again, and I'm—looks like I'm going for another 1996 Olympic Games, Atlanta, probably the most exciting one for the United States. That's because Kim Zmeskal, my late World Champion, she has decided to go for another one . . . and I'm going to stay behind her.

"That's probably the most interesting, and at the same time is the most weird human story I ever had in my thirty-five years of coaching career," Bela said of Kim's career. "One of mightiness to get the highest extent of the athletic life, being the very first World Champion for the United States, then, unexpectedly, it falls apart . . . because the expectation was so high. Then she has the strength, and she has the moral ability to come back, and I think it is beautiful."[44]

Kim graduated from Westfield High School on Saturday, June 4, 1994. She decided to put her college plans on hold, however, in order to train.

In Worcester, Massachusetts, on June 10, Kim declared formally that she wanted to compete again. When asked if she had someone good to train her, she laughed and said that Bela Karolyi had also come out of retirement and he would be coaching her.

"I spent many nights not knowing what to do and praying that someone would please just tell me," Kim said about her two-year hiatus from competitive gymnastics. "But it all came down to that I still enjoyed doing the sport of gymnastics and that I feel like I have more to offer. I think that I could give something to the U.S. team and I've always been a competitive person and the exhibitions have been really great these past couple of years, but there's just been a hole inside of me that hasn't been able to be filled with anything that competition did."[45]

Kim began her tough road back into competitive gymnastics with an exhibition floor routine at the 1994 USA versus Romania meet during the preliminary competition. Her appearance had changed a little; she was now eighteen years old, taller, and a little heavier. Her smile revealed braces on her teeth, but she showed she was the same Kim of old, executing her patented three whip backs into a lofty double back. There were not many people in the audience to witness her routine, but Bela was there to once again instruct and encourage her.

"[It's] going to be a hard, rocky road, no doubt about it," Bela acknowledged regarding Kim's decision to make a comeback. "We've been talking, and I made very, very clear what she can expect for. But she is a very smart, very bright, and extremely determined young lady."[46]

"I am fortunate to have Bela and Martha Karolyi as coaches,"[47] Kim said gratefully.

"I know better than anybody else how difficult the road is gonna be," Bela said. "And I know the details and all the ingredients of an effort, of a challenge to respond to the kind of challenge what we are taking now. And I talk with her, 'Remember all those times. Remember the struggle. Remember all the ingredients which were involved, good and bad.'"[48]

Bela wanted to make sure Kim fully appreciated the challenge ahead. "I did not want to talk her out of it," he said. "But I did want to make sure she understands what she's talking about . . . the hard workouts . . . the long hours of preparation . . . and also, I didn't want to give her any chance to think she's gonna be celebrated out on the floor with a red carpet rolled out for her . . . because [in 1992] she had a position, she had a status. But now she has no status."

Having taken time off, some of Kim's persistent injuries had healed and she had enjoyed a welcome mental break from the stressful and demanding schedule a top gymnast must endure. But as old injuries healed, new ones seemed to be cropping up. She was noticeably favoring her right leg as she walked around at the USA versus Romania team final. She did not see the entire competition because she left the arena to ice her hyper-extended right knee which had been injured during her floor exhibition the previous day. When a doctor looked at her knee, he informed her that she had torn her anterior cruciate ligament and would need surgery. Kim agreed to the surgery and began rehabilitation shortly after. Clearly, her comeback battle would not be easy.

"I think a lot of it's gonna have to be smart training," Kim said, realizing that gymnastics would be more difficult this time around. "I don't feel like I'm eighteen. I haven't had the growth spurt, so I've been lucky with that. But, of course, I'm gonna have to be a lot more careful."

Kim was embarking on a new journey, the challenge of making a successful comeback. Many had tried—Mark Spitz, Kurt Thomas, Brandy Johnson, Katarina Witt, Brian Boitano— but they had not been able to match their previous accomplishments. However, they had regained their competitive form—a remarkable achievement in itself. Kim not only had to recapture the shape she had been in during the 1992 Olympics, but she needed to go one step further and improve her routines in order to compete with the younger gymnasts who were continually increasing the amount of difficulty in their routines. Kim would need a lot of courage and steadfastness to endure the long hours in the gym, and she would again have to make the sacrifices needed to focus completely on gymnastics.

"Mentally, I think about things a lot differently and things seem more important to me," Kim said. "I think to make World Championship teams or Olympic teams would be a lot more special this time around."[49]

Kim said that her problems in Barcelona still haunted her to this day. Maybe Atlanta would offer a second chance at her Olympic dream.

By the time the 1996 Olympics roll around, Kim will be twenty years old. By today's standards that may be old for a gymnast. But others have succeeded despite their age. Kathy Johnson was twenty-four in the 1984 Olympics, and Kelly Garrison was twenty-one in the 1988 Olympics. Elena Shushunova was nineteen when she won the 1988 Olympics, and Svetlana Boginskaya was nineteen in Barcelona. Also, Shannon Miller is hoping to hang on until 1996 when she will be nineteen.

Bela had always thought an Olympics hosted in the United States would provide a strong advantage. "To have the Olympic Games in your own country is such a fantastic opportunity," he had once said enthusiastically. "I would stand on my head and spit quarters for that chance."[50]

Kim might just get that chance. Perhaps the outcome will be the same as it was for her idol Mary Lou.

Kim will return to the competitive arena in search of the only title that eluded her, that of Olympic Champion. Whatever happens, Kim Zmeskal has definitely left her mark on the sport of women's gymnastics and will always be remembered as the first American to ever win the all-around in a World Championships. Maybe she will join the ranks of Olga, Nadia, and Mary Lou and also win an Olympic gold medal.

* * *

Remember that tenacious little fighter on the balance beam? She is back, only now she is a mature woman. She again subjects herself to rigorous repetitions under the watchful eye of her coaches. She bends, twists, and flips her body like before. She holds a handstand while her back bends so far that it looks as though it will break in half.

Her calf muscles bulge, her hands reveal thick calluses from years of uneven bar work, and her body is defined from long hours of conditioning like that of a sculpture chiseled by an artist. She wears wrist guards on both arms that provide a reminder of past injuries.

She is now the one whom the cameras follow, the one whom little children stare at and hope to be like someday. She again enjoys the challenge of trying to be the best in the world. Of trying to be perfect. And her goal is still the same: to win a gold medal in the Olympics.

She has the soul of a tiger, and her competitive flame still burns brightly with the determination to win.

KIM ZMESKAL

1989 Junior National Champion
American Classic Winner
Swiss Cup Mixed Pairs Champion
Arthur Gander Memorial Winner
City of Popes Winner

1990 Peachtree Classic Winner
American Cup Champion
International Mixed Pairs Champion
United States Challenge Winner
U.S. Senior National Champion
USA versus USSR Champion

1991 Alamo City Invitational Winner
International Mixed Pairs Champion
USA versus Romania Champion
U.S. Senior National Champion
World Champion: All-Around

1992 Alamo City Invitational Winner
American Cup Champion
World Champion: Beam, Floor
U.S. Senior National Champion
Olympic Bronze Medalist: Team

1993 World Open Winner

The *First* American (Male or Female) to Win the World Championships in the All-Around

188

NOTES

Chapter 1 THE LITTLE TIGER

1. *International Gymnast*, October 1989, p. 14.
2. *International Gymnast*, December 1990, p. 32.
3. WTBS, 1990 Goodwill Games: Team Final, aired on July 27, 1990.
4. Richard O'Brien, "Lord Gym," *Sports Illustrated*, July 27, 1992, pp. 48-50.
5. *USA Gymnastics*, November/December 1993, p. 37.
6. ESPN, 1990 McDonald's International Mixed Pairs, aired on March 18, 1990.
7. Bela Karolyi and Nancy Ann Richardson, <u>Feel No Fear: The Power, Passion, & Politics of a Life in Gymnastics</u>. Hyperion: 1994, p. 191.
8. ESPN, 1990 McDonald's International Mixed Pairs, aired on March 18, 1990.
9. WTBS, 1990 Goodwill Games: Team Final, aired on July 27, 1990.
10. ABC, 1991 World Championships: Event Finals, aired on September 15, 1991.
11. *USA Gymnastics*, January/February 1994, p. 27.
12. *International Gymnast*, December 1990, p. 32.
13. *International Gymnast*, December 1991, p. 21.
14. *International Gymnast*, December 1990, p. 32.
15. *International Gymnast*, October 1993, p. 58.
16. NBC *SportsWorld*, 1990 U.S. Championships: Event Finals, aired on June 17, 1990.
17. NBC *Olympic Showcase*, 1991 McDonald's American Cup, aired on February 23, 1991.
18. *International Gymnast*, December 1990, pp. 32, 40.
19. Richard O'Brien, "Lord Gym," *Sports Illustrated*, July 27, 1992, p. 52.
20. NBC, 1992 Summer Olympics: All-Around Preview, aired on July 29, 1992.
21. ABC *Wide World of Sports*, 1990 McDonald's Challenge: USA versus USSR, aired on August 4, 1990.
22. *International Gymnast*, December 1990, pp. 32, 40.
23. NBC *SportsWorld*, 1990 U.S. Championships, aired on June 16, 1990.
24. Jill Smolowe, "Don't Call Them Pixies," *Time*, July 27, 1992, p. 58.
25. NBC *Olympic Showcase*, 1991 U.S. Championships, aired on June 15, 1991.
26. *International Gymnast*, December 1990, pp. 32, 40.
27. NBC *Olympic Showcase*, 1992 Phar-Mor U.S. Championships, aired on May 23, 1992.
28. *International Gymnast*, August 1988, p. 31.

29. *International Gymnast*, September 1988, pp. 22, 39.

Chapter 2 BEATING THE COMPETITION
1. *USA Gymnastics*, November/December 1993, p. 37.
2. Jill Smolowe, "Don't Call Them Pixies," *Time*, July 27, 1992, p. 58.
3. *International Gymnast*, December 1990, p. 32.
4. ESPN, 1989 Olympic Sports Festival, aired on July 28, 1989.
5. *USA Gymnastics*, September/October 1993, p. 37.
6. *International Gymnast*, October 1989, p. 13.
7. ESPN, 1989 Olympic Sports Festival, aired on July 28, 1989.
8. *International Gymnast*, April 1994, p. 9.
9. *International Gymnast*, October 1989, p. 14.
10. *International Gymnast*, March 1990, p. 10.
11. *International Gymnast*, December 1990, p. 32.
12. ESPN, 1990 McDonald's International Mixed Pairs, aired on March 18, 1990.
13. NBC *Olympic Showcase*, 1991 International Challenge: USA versus Romania, aired on April 16, 1991.
14. ESPN, 1990 McDonald's International Mixed Pairs, aired on March 18, 1990.
15. *International Gymnast*, May 1990, p. 15.
16. ESPN, 1990 McDonald's International Mixed Pairs, aired on March 18, 1990.
17. *International Gymnast*, May 1990, p. 15.
18. *International Gymnast*, February 1991, p. 34.
19. ESPN, 1990 McDonald's International Mixed Pairs, aired on March 18, 1990.
20. *International Gymnast*, May 1990, p. 20.
21. ESPN, 1990 McDonald's International Mixed Pairs, aired on March 18, 1990.
22. *International Gymnast*, May 1990, p. 20.
23. *International Gymnast*, December 1990, p. 33.
24. *International Gymnast*, June 1990, pp. 17-21, 47.
25. NBC, 1992 Summer Olympics: Team Final, aired on July 28, 1992.
26. *International Gymnast*, December 1990, p. 40.
27. *USA Gymnastics*, May/June 1990, p. 16.
28. *International Gymnast*, December 1990, p. 32.
29. Bela Karolyi and Nancy Ann Richardson, <u>Feel No Fear: The Power, Passion, & Politics of a Life in Gymnastics</u>. Hyperion, 1994, p. 193.
30. ABC *Wide World of Sports*, 1990 McDonald's Challenge: USA versus USSR, aired on August 4, 1990.
31. ABC *Wide World of Sports*, 1990 McDonald's Challenge: USA versus USSR, aired on August 4, 1990.

32. WTBS, 1990 Goodwill Games: Team Final, aired on July 27, 1990.
33. *International Gymnast*, December 1990, pp. 33, 40.

Chapter 3 THE NATIONAL CHAMPION
1. *International Gymnast*, August/September 1991, p. 10.
2. NBC, 1992 Summer Olympics: All-Around Final, aired on July 30, 1992.
3. NBC *SportsWorld*, 1990 U.S. Championships, aired on June 16, 1990.
4. WTBS, 1990 Goodwill Games: Team Final, aired on July 27, 1990.
5. *International Gymnast*, September 1990, p. 38.
6. NBC *SportsWorld*, 1990 U.S. Championships, aired on June 16, 1990.
7. *International Gymnast*, September 1990, pp. 9, 18.
8. WTBS, 1990 Goodwill Games: Team Final, aired on July 27, 1990.
9. *International Gymnast*, October 1990, p. 18.
10. WTBS, 1990 Goodwill Games: All-Around Final, aired on July 28, 1990.
11. WTBS, 1990 Goodwill Games: Team Final, aired on July 27, 1990.
12. *International Gymnast*, October 1990, p. 18.
13. WTBS, 1990 Goodwill Games: All-Around Final, aired on July 28, 1990.
14. *International Gymnast*, October 1990, p. 20.
15. *USA Gymnastics*, November/December 1990, p. 24.
16. *International Gymnast*, October 1990, p. 20.
17. *International Gymnast*, December 1990, p. 33.
18. *International Gymnast*, October 1990, p. 21.
19. WTBS, 1990 Goodwill Games: All-Around Final, aired on July 28, 1990.
20. *International Gymnast*, October 1990, p. 21.
21. WTBS, 1990 Goodwill Games: Event Finals, aired on July 29, 1990.
22. *International Gymnast*, April 1994, p. 9.
23. WTBS, 1990 Goodwill Games: Event Finals, aired on July 29, 1990.
24. *International Gymnast*, November 1990, p. 34.
25. *International Gymnast*, December 1990, p. 40.
26. ABC *Wide World of Sports*, 1990 McDonald's Challenge: USA versus USSR, aired on August 4, 1990.
27. ABC *Wide World of Sports*, 1990 McDonald's Challenge: USA versus USSR, aired on August 4, 1990.
28. ABC *Wide World of Sports*, 1990 McDonald's Challenge: USA versus USSR, aired on August 4, 1990.
29. *International Gymnast*, December 1990, p. 40.
30. *International Gymnast*, November 1990, pp. 34, 38.
31. NBC *Olympic Showcase*, 1992 Olympic Trials aired, on June 13, 1992.

Chapter 4 PROBLEMS WITH BELA
1. *International Gymnast*, April 1994, p. 11.
2. *USA Gymnastics*, March/April 1991, p. 28.
3. *International Gymnast*, April 1991, pp. 22-24.

191

4. ABC, 1992 Individual Apparatus World Championships, aired on April 25, 1992.
5. *International Gymnast*, May 1991, p. 10.
6. NBC *Olympic Showcase*, 1991 McDonald's American Cup, aired on February 23, 1991.
7. *International Gymnast*, April 1994, p. 12.
8. NBC, 1992 Summer Olympics: All-Around Preview, aired on July 29, 1992.
9. NBC *Olympic Showcase*, 1991 McDonald's American Cup, aired on February 23, 1991.
10. *International Gymnast*, May 1991, p. 18.
11. ESPN, 1991 McDonald's International Mixed Pairs, aired on March 16, 1991.
12. NBC *Olympic Showcase*, 1991 International Challenge: USA versus Romania aired on April 16, 1991.
13. *International Gymnast*, June/July 1991, p. 34.
14. NBC *Olympic Showcase*, 1991 International Challenge: USA versus Romania, aired on April 16, 1991.
15. *USA Gymnastics*, March/April 1994, p. 37.
16. Richard O'Brien, "Lord Gym," *Sports Illustrated*, July 27, 1992, p. 52.
17. NBC *Olympic Showcase*, 1991 U.S. Championships, aired on June 15, 1991.
18. ESPN, Superstars of Gymnastics, aired on November 29, 1993.
19. *USA Gymnastics*, September/October 1993, p. 37.
20. NBC *Olympic Showcase*, 1991 U.S. Championships, aired on June 15, 1991.
21. NBC *Olympic Showcase*, 1991 U.S. Championships: Event Finals, aired on June 16, 1991.
22. NBC, 1992 Summer Olympics: Team Final, aired on July 28, 1992.
23. ABC *Wide World of Sports*, 1991 World Championships: All-Around Final, aired on February 29, 1992.
24. *International Gymnast*, December 1990, p. 33.
25. ABC, 1991 World Championships: Event Finals, aired on September 14, 1991.
26. *International Gymnast*, December 1990, p. 40.
27. ABC, 1991 World Championships: Event Finals, aired on September 14, 1991.
28. Barbara Kantrowitz with Mark Starr, "Living With Training," *Newsweek*, August 10, 1992, p. 24.
29. *International Gymnast*, August/September 1991, p. 10.

Chapter 5 CONQUERING THE WORLD

1. *International Gymnast*, August/September 1991, p. 10.
2. ESPN, 1991 World Championships: Team Final, aired on October 18, 1991.
3. *International Gymnast*, December 1990, p. 32.

4. *International Gymnast*, November 1991, pp. 19, 23.
5. ESPN, 1991 World Championships: Team Final, aired on October 18, 1991.
6. *International Gymnast*, November 1991, p. 24.
7. ABC *Wide World of Sports*, 1991 World Championships: All-Around Final, aired on February 29, 1992.
8. *International Gymnast*, November 1991, p. 24.
9. ESPN, 1991 World Championships: Team Final, aired on October 18, 1991.
10. *International Gymnast*, November 1991, p. 24.
11. ESPN, 1991 World Championships: Team Final, aired on October 18, 1991.
12. *International Gymnast*, November 1991, p. 24.
13. ABC, 1991 World Championships: Event Finals, aired on September 15, 1991.
14. ABC, 1991 World Championships: Event Finals, aired on September 14, 1991.
15. *International Gymnast*, April 1994, p. 9.
16. ABC, 1991 World Championships: Event Finals, aired on September 14, 1991.
17. *International Gymnast*, April 1994, p. 10.
18. *International Gymnast*, May 1992, p. 48.
19. ABC, 1991 World Championships: Event Finals, aired on September 14, 1991.
20. ABC *Wide World of Sports*, 1991 World Championships: All-Around Final, aired on February 29, 1992.
21. *International Gymnast*, April 1994, p. 10.
22. *International Gymnast*, December 1991, p. 21.
23. *International Gymnast*, April 1994, pp. 9-10.
24. NBC *Olympic Showcase*, 1992 Olympic Trials, aired on June 13, 1992.
25. Richard O'Brien, "Lord Gym," *Sports Illustrated*, July 27, 1992, p. 47.
26. ABC *Wide World of Sports*, 1991 World Championships: All-Around Final, aired on February 29, 1992.
27. *International Gymnast*, December 1991, p. 21.
28. *International Gymnast*, May 1992, p. 10.
29. ABC, 1991 World Championships: Event Finals, aired on September 14, 1991.
30. ABC, 1991 World Championships: Event Finals, aired on September 15, 1991.
31. *International Gymnast*, December 1991, p. 22.
32. ABC, 1991 World Championships: Event Finals, aired on September 15, 1991.
33. *International Gymnast*, May 1992, p. 38.
34. *International Gymnast*, March 1992, p. 46.
35. *USA Gymnastics*, March/April 1992, p. 18.
36. *International Gymnast*, April 1993, p. 37.

37. Bela Karolyi and Nancy Ann Richardson, <u>Feel No Fear: The Power, Passion, & Politics of a Life in Gymnastics</u>. Hyperion: 1994, p. 208.

Chapter 6 SILENCING THE SKEPTICS
1. ABC, 1992 Individual Apparatus World Championships, aired on April 19, 1992.
2. *USA Gymnastics*, March/April 1994, p. 36.
3. ABC, 1992 Individual Apparatus World Championships, aired on April 19, 1992.
4. WTBS, 1990 Goodwill Games: Team Final, aired on July 27, 1990.
5. NBC *Olympic Showcase*, 1992 McDonald's American Cup, aired on March 7, 1992.
6. *International Gymnast*, May 1992, p. 32.
7. NBC *Olympic Showcase*, 1992 McDonald's American Cup, aired on March 7, 1992.
8. *International Gymnast*, May 1992, p. 11.
9. NBC *Olympic Showcase*, 1992 McDonald's American Cup, aired on March 7, 1992.
10. ESPN, 1992 McDonald's International Mixed Pairs, aired on March 19, 1992.
11. WTBS *U.S. Olympic Gold*, 1992 Hilton's Superstars of Gymnastics, aired on July 18, 1992.
12. Bela Karolyi and Nancy Ann Richardson, <u>Feel No Fear: The Power, Passion, & Politics of a Life in Gymnastics</u>. Hyperion, 1994, pp. 209-210.
13. ABC, 1992 Individual Apparatus World Championships, aired on April 25, 1992.
14. *International Gymnast*, June/July 1992, p. 11.
15. *International Gymnast*, March 1991, p. 48.
16. ABC, 1992 Individual Apparatus World Championships, aired on April 19, 1992.
17. *International Gymnast*, June/July 1992, p. 11.
18. ABC, 1992 Individual Apparatus World Championships, aired on April 19, 1992.

Chapter 7 MAKING THE DREAM TEAM
1. NBC *Olympic Showcase*, 1992 Phar-Mor U.S. Championships, aired on May 23, 1992.
2. *USA Gymnastics*, July/August 1992, p. 23.
3. NBC *Olympic Showcase*, 1992 Phar-Mor U.S. Championships, aired on May 23, 1992.
4. *International Gymnast*, April 1994, p. 11.
5. *USA Gymnastics*, July/August 1992, p. 24.

6. NBC *Olympic Showcase*, 1992 Phar-Mor U.S. Championships, aired on May 23, 1992.
7. Bela Karolyi and Nancy Ann Richardson, <u>Feel No Fear: The Power, Passion, & Politics of a Life in Gymnastics</u>. Hyperion: 1994, p. 211.
8. Richard O'Brien, "Lord Gym," *Sports Illustrated*, July 27, 1992, p. 52.
9. NBC *SportsWorld*, 1990 U.S. Championships, aired on June 16, 1990.
10. Richard O'Brien, "Lord Gym," *Sports Illustrated*, July 27, 1992, p. 52.
11. Skip Hollandsworth, "Bela Karolyi: I Have Made Their Lives Miserable," *Texas Monthly*, December 1991, p. 146-149, 184-192.
12. NBC, 1992 Summer Olympics: Gymnastics Preview, aired on July 25, 1992.
13. ABC, 1992 Individual Apparatus World Championships, aired on April 19, 1992.
14. NBC *Olympic Showcase*, 1992 Olympic Trials, aired on June 13, 1992.
15. *International Gymnast*, August/September 1992, p. 24.
16. NBC *Olympic Showcase*, 1992 Olympic Trials, aired on June 13, 1992.
17. *International Gymnast*, August/September 1991, pp. 10, 26.
18. Steve Wieberg, "Gymnastics Rivalry Full of Twists," *USA Today*, July 24, 1992, p. 2C.
19. *International Gymnast*, August/September 1992, pp. 27, 30, 48, 59.
20. NBC, 1992 Summer Olympics: Team Final, aired on July 28, 1992.
21. NBC, *Faith Daniels*, aired on August 27, 1992.
22. *International Gymnast*, April 1994, p. 11.
23. NBC, 1992 Summer Olympics: Preview, aired on July 24, 1992.
24. Richard O'Brien, "Lord Gym," *Sports Illustrated*, July 27, 1992, p. 47.
25. *International Gymnast*, October 1992, p. 7.
26. *International Gymnast*, April 1994, p. 11.
27. *International Gymnast*, August/September 1991, p. 10.
28. Bela Karolyi and Nancy Ann Richardson, <u>Feel No Fear: The Power, Passion, & Politics of a Life in Gymnastics</u>. Hyperion: 1994, p. 215.

Chapter 8 THE FALL
1. NBC *Olympic Showcase*, 1992 Olympic Trials, aired on June 13, 1992.
2. *International Gymnast*, April 1994, p. 10.
3. NBC *Olympic Showcase*, 1992 Phar-Mor U.S. Championships, aired on May 23, 1992.
4. Jill Smolowe, "Don't Call Them Pixies," *Time*, July 27, 1992, p. 58.
5. *International Gymnast*, April 1994, p. 10.
6. Steve Wieberg, "Gymnastics Rivalry Full of Twists," *USA Today*, July 24, 1992, p. 2C.
7. NBC, 1992 Summer Olympics: Gymnastics Preview, aired on July 25, 1992.
8. Jill Smolowe, "Don't Call Them Pixies," *Time*, July 27, 1992, p. 58.

9. Tom Weir, "Gritty Zmeskal Regains Footing," *USA Today*, July 29, 1992, p. 3E.
10. Jerry Adler and Mark Starr, "Flying High Now," *Newsweek*, August 10, 1992, p. 20.
11. NBC, 1992 Summer Olympics: Team Compulsories, aired on July 26, 1992.
12. Tom Weir, "Gritty Zmeskal Regains Footing," *USA Today*, July 29, 1992, p. 3E.
13. *International Gymnast*, April 1994, p. 10.
14. Tom Weir, "Gritty Zmeskal Regains Footing," *USA Today*, July 29, 1992, p. 3E.
15. ABC, 1992 Individual Apparatus World Championships, aired on April 25, 1992.
16. *International Gymnast*, August/September 1992, p. 34.
17. Tom Weir, "Gritty Zmeskal Regains Footing," *USA Today*, July 29, 1992, p. 3E.
18. NBC, 1992 Summer Olympics: Team Final, aired on July 28, 1992.
19. Steve Wieberg, "Miller Showing World She's Back in Charge," *USA Today*, July 29, 1992, p. 3E.
20. *International Gymnast*, October 1992, p. 14.
21. "Zmeskal Zooms into Contention for All-Around Title," *USA Today*, July 29, 1992, p. 3E.
22. Steve Wieberg, "Individuals Overshadow Team Bronze," *USA Today*, July 29, 1992, p. 3E.
23. NBC, 1992 Summer Olympics: Team Final, aired on July 28, 1992.
24. *International Gymnast*, November 1992, p. 26.
25. *International Gymnast*, April 1994, p. 12.

Chapter 9 BATTLE FOR THE GOLD

1. ABC *Wide World of Sports*, 1991 World Championships: All-Around Final, aired on February 29, 1992.
2. NBC, 1992 Summer Olympics: All-Around Final, aired on July 30, 1992.
3. *International Gymnast*, October 1992, p. 26.
4. *International Gymnast*, April 1994, p. 11.
5. *International Gymnast*, April 1993, p. 30.
6. *International Gymnast*, April 1994, p. 14.
7. NBC, 1992 Summer Olympics: All-Around Final, aired on July 30, 1992.
8. *International Gymnast*, December 1992, p. 33.
9. NBC, 1992 Summer Olympics: All-Around Final, aired on July 30, 1992.
10. *International Gymnast*, October 1992, p. 29.
11. *International Gymnast*, April 1994, p. 10.
12. NBC, *Faith Daniels*, aired on August 27, 1992.
13. NBC, *Faith Daniels*, aired on August 27, 1992.

14. Bela Karolyi and Nancy Ann Richardson, <u>Feel No Fear: The Power, Passion, & Politics of a Life in Gymnastics</u>. Hyperion: 1994, p. 217.
15. NBC, 1992 Summer Olympics: Event Finals, aired on August 1, 1992.
16. *International Gymnast*, October 1992, p. 54.
17. *International Gymnast*, April 1994, p. 10.
18. *International Gymnast*, May 1993, p. 44.
19. *International Gymnast*, April 1994, p. 10.
20. *International Gymnast*, November 1992, p. 26.
21. *International Gymnast*, April 1994, p. 10.
22. Jill Smolowe, "Don't Call Them Pixies," *Time*, July 27, 1992, p. 58.

Chapter 10 A COMEBACK
1. Aric Press, "Old Too Soon, Wise Too Late?" *Newsweek*, August 10, 1992 pp. 22-23.
2. *International Gymnast*, April 1994, p. 12.
3. ABC, 1993 World Championships: Event Finals, aired on April 25, 1993.
4. *International Gymnast*, April 1994, pp. 11-12.
5. *USA Gymnastics*, November/December 1993, p. 37.
6. *International Gymnast*, February 1993, p. 38.
7. *International Gymnast*, April 1994, p. 12.
8. *International Gymnast*, March 1993, p. 48.
9. *International Gymnast*, May 1993, p. 20.
10. *International Gymnast*, April 1994, p. 12.
11. *International Gymnast*, May 1993, p. 44.
12. NBC, 1993 Coca-Cola U.S. Championships, aired on August 28, 1993.
13. Bela Karolyi and Nancy Ann Richardson, <u>Feel No Fear: The Power, Passion, & Politics of a Life in Gymnastics</u>. Hyperion: 1994, pp. 219-220.
14. *USA Gymnastics*, September/October 1993, p. 37.
15. *USA Gymnastics*, March/April 1994, p. 37.
16. *International Gymnast*, April 1994, p. 14.
17. Jill Smolowe, "Don't Call Them Pixies," *Time*, July 27, 1992, p. 58.
18. *USA Gymnastics*, March/April 1994, pp. 14, 37.
19. *USA Gymnastics*, November/December 1993, p. 45.
20. *USA Gymnastics*, March/April 1994, p. 37.
21. *USA Gymnastics*, November/December 1993, p. 45.
22. *USA Gymnastics*, March/April 1994, p. 24.
23. *International Gymnast*, April 1994, pp. 12, 14.
24. *USA Gymnastics*, May/June 1994, p. 36.
25. *International Gymnast*, May 1994, p. 40.
26. *International Gymnast*, April 1994, p. 14.
27. Skip Hollandsworth, "Bela Karolyi: I Have Made Their Lives Miserable," *Texas Monthly*, December 1991, p. 146-149, 184-192.
28. NBC, 1992 Summer Olympics: Team Final, aired on July 28, 1992.

29. Barbara Kantrowitz with Mark Starr, "Living With Training," *Newsweek*, August 10, 1992, p. 25.
30. NBC, 1992 Summer Olympics: Team Final, aired on July 28, 1992.
31. Barbara Kantrowitz with Mark Starr, "Living With Training," *Newsweek*, August 10, 1992, p. 25.
32. Richard O'Brien, "Lord Gym," *Sports Illustrated*, July 27, 1992, p. 48.
33. Skip Hollandsworth, "Bela Karolyi: I Have Made Their Lives Miserable," *Texas Monthly*, December 1991, p. 146-149, 184-192.
34. Richard O'Brien, "Lord Gym," *Sports Illustrated*, July 27, 1992, p. 47.
35. *International Gymnast*, April 1994, pp. 10, 14.
36. *International Gymnast*, March 1994, p. 26.
37. Bela Karolyi and Nancy Ann Richardson, Feel No Fear: The Power, Passion, & Politics of a Life in Gymnastics. Hyperion: 1994, pp. 196-197.
38. ESPN, 1991 World Championships: Team Final, aired on October 18, 1991.
39. *International Gymnast*, December 1990, p. 40.
40. NBC, 1993 Coca-Cola U.S. Championships, aired on August 28, 1993.
41. *International Gymnast*, April 1994, pp. 12, 14.
42. *International Gymnast*, October 1993, p. 58.
43. *International Gymnast*, August/September 1994, p. 48.
44. ABC, *Good Morning America*, aired on May 25, 1994.
45. NBC *SportsWorld*, 1994 Budget Rent A Car Invitational: USA versus Romania, aired on June 19, 1994.
46. ABC, *Good Morning America*, aired on May 25, 1994.
47. *USA Gymnastics*, May/June 1994, p. 36.
48. NBC *SportsWorld*, 1994 Budget Rent A Car Invitational: USA versus Romania, aired on June 19, 1994.
49. *International Gymnast*, August/September 1994, pp. 48-49.
50. Mary Lou Retton, Bela Karolyi, John Powers, Mary Lou: Creating An Olympic Champion. McGraw-Hill Book Company: 1986, p. 167.

Unless otherwise indicated in the text, these notes apply to quotations without superscript numbers in immediately preceding paragraphs.

ABOUT THE AUTHOR

Krista Quiner is an author of several gymnastics biographies, including *Dominique Moceanu: A Gymnastics Sensation* and *Shannon Miller: America's Most Decorated Gymnast*. She grew up in Medina, Ohio, and now resides in New Jersey with her husband and daughter. Formerly known as Krista Bailey, she was a competitive gymnast for fifteen years. She began her gymnastics career at Gymnastics World in Broadview Heights, Ohio. She competed as a Class I gymnast at Gymnastics of Ohio in North Canton throughout high school and received a gymnastics scholarship to the University of Denver, an NCAA Division I school, where she set a school record on floor exercise. Krista holds a Bachelor's degree from the University of Denver in International Studies and in French.

FOR FURTHER READING:

Dominique Moceanu: A Gymnastics Sensation
Written by Krista Quiner
Published by The Bradford Book Company in 1997

Shannon Miller: America's Most Decorated Gymnast
Written by Krista Quiner
Published by The Bradford Book Company in 1997

Landing On My Feet: A Diary of Dreams
Written by Kerri Strug with John Lopez
Published by Andrews McMeel Publishing in 1997

Romanian Gymnastics
Written by Kurt Treptow
Published by The Center for Romanian Studies in 1996

FOR CHILDREN'S READING:

Trent Dimas: Gold Medal Olympic Gymnast
Written by Valerie Menard and Sue Boulais
Published by Mitchell Lane Publishers in 1998

Superstars of Women's Gymnastics
Written by Joel Cohen
Published by Chelsea House Publishers in 1997

Kerri Strug: Heart of Gold
Written by Kerri Strug with Greg Brown
Published by Taylor Publishing in 1996